200 SKILLS EVERY COOK MUST HAVE

200 SKILLS EVERY COOK MUST HAVE

**The Step-by-step Methods
That Will Turn a Good Cook
Into a Great Cook**

CLARA PAUL and ERIC TREUILLÉ

FIREFLY BOOKS

A FIREFLY BOOK

Published by Firefly Books Ltd. 2013

First printing

Publisher Cataloging-in-Publication Data (U.S.)

Paul, Clara.
    200 skills every cook must have : the step-by-step methods that will turn a good cook into a great cook / Clara Paul and Eric Treuille
[256] p. : col. photos. ;   cm.
Includes index.
ISBN-13: 978-1-77085-210-5
1. Cooking. 2. Cookbooks. I. Treuille, Eric. II Title. III.
Two hundred skills every cook must have.
641. 5 dc23   TX714.P374 2013

Library and Archives Canada Cataloguing in Publication

A CIP record for this title is available from Library and Archives Canada

Published in the United States by
Firefly Books (U.S.) Inc.
P.O. Box 1338, Ellicott Station
Buffalo, New York 14205

Published in Canada by
Firefly Books Ltd.
50 Staples Avenue, Unit 1
Richmond Hill, Ontario L4B 0A7

Cover design: Erin R. Holmes/Soplari Design
Interior design: Lindsey Johns

Printed in China

This book was conceived, designed and produced by
Quintet Publishing Limited
6 Blundell Street
London N7 9BH
United Kingdom

For Quintet:

Photographer **Jon Whitaker**
Designer **Anna Gatt**
Art Director **Michael Charles**
Managing Editor **Emma Bastow**
Editor **Julie Brooke**
Publisher **Mark Searle**

CONTENTS

INTRODUCTION

Books for Cooks in London, England has been sourcing, stocking, and selling a vast range of cookbooks to a loyal customer base since it first opened its doors in 1983. From very early on, the store has featured a tiny testing kitchen, where recipes from the books are put through their paces and sampled by appreciative customers in the little dining area at the back of the store.

This enviable yet challenging role is currently the responsibility of Clara Paul and Eric Treuillé who have been working together at Books for Cooks for the last four years. During that time they have encountered cookbooks of all shapes and sizes on every kind of cuisine, ingredient, food trend, and style imaginable. The culinary duo spend their days "cooking the books" so to speak, as they peruse the hundreds of cookbooks that line the store's shelves and select a different menu to cook every lunchtime.

CREATIVE COOKING

Although they are literally surrounded by wall-to-wall inspiration, it takes a clever cook to instinctively know the extent of their skills, the limitations of time, a diminutive kitchen, and the culinary preferences of their customers. However, Clara and Eric rise to the challenge and continue to create a varied and exciting daily menu, which is why Books for Cooks has become the most exclusive place to lunch in Notting Hill, one of London's trendiest neighborhoods.

BOOKING A PLACE ON THE SHELVES

With their combined knowledge and experience of cookbooks and recipe testing, the pair wanted to create a book that would help people get more out of their own recipe books, learning the necessary skills and techniques needed to attempt more of the recipes, rather than flipping through and looking wistfully at recipes they feel are beyond their skills and experience.

Clara and Eric believe that every bookshelf needs the ultimate book that answers all the queries, questions, and uncertainties that every home cook has, however experienced or confident they might be. They felt that the range of skills and techniques needed to be updated and demystified, bringing a more modern and contemporary approach to the basic techniques that are the building blocks of all cooking.

It was important to make these skills relevant to current styles of cooking, along with the budgets, ingredients and trends that make up the culinary world as we now know it. They also wanted to inject some enthusiasm and fun into those techniques that perhaps seem somewhat dated or obsolete, bringing some classic skills back into the kitchen and reintroducing home cooks to ingredients that seem old-fashioned or are more often bought ready prepared.

THE IMPORTANCE OF BASIC SKILLS

Skills and techniques are the foundation of all cooking, however, they are not dependent on years of training, qualifications or skills – they are grounded in practice, confidence and knowledge.

Cooking techniques are about executing something in the right way in order to achieve the best results while doing so in the most efficient manner. This could be something as simple as changing the piece of equipment you have been using or the method you use, or even altering the order in which you tackle whatever it is you may be cooking. What is important is approaching the task armed with the right information and the right tools to ensure you work in the most efficient way possible.

Cooking is as much about pleasure and fun as it is about precision and perfection. Knowing the best way to execute a recipe is an essential part of the process, and having the skills at your fingertips is the place to start from. This clear, uncomplicated book provides a step-by-step guide to the whole process.

USING THIS BOOK

Clara and Eric have written a book that is a guide to terminology and culinary phrasing; a dictionary for all that happens in the kitchen. This book aims to give you better results with less effort and – most importantly – to give you the maximum enjoyment and fulfilment from all your cooking endeavors.

The book is divided into 12 chapters, each focusing on a key set of skills or a type of food or ingredient. The easy-to-use layout lists all the utensils and ingredients you will need to

practice each skill, followed by detailed steps to guide you through the technique. Expert tips offer handy advice on alternative methods, explanations of terms, and additional techniques for when you gain more confidence. The steps are all easy to follow, so you will be able to master any skill, whether you are a novice or a well practiced home cook. There is also a handy equipment list, as well as a glossary of all the culinary terms you are likely to come across as you work through your cookbook collection and try new recipes.

By the time you have finished reading this book you will know how to do everything from stone an avocado and blanch an almond, to fillet a fish, truss a chicken and shuck an oyster. With this essential collection of culinary skills at your fingertips, your kitchen confidence will grow in leaps and bounds. Dishes such as dressed crab and rack of lamb will no longer be saved for restaurant outings – they will become dinner table favorites in your own home.

As with all skills, practice makes perfect. Keep this book by your side in the kitchen and every challenge will become a new culinary possibility; every technique mastered will increase your repertoire and your confidence.

ESSENTIAL EQUIPMENT

If you are serious about learning the basic skills needed to confidently cook a whole range of recipes, you will need a well stocked kitchen. While many techniques and recipes call for a limited number of pans and utensils – and for many others there are alternatives – certain techniques require specific pieces of kitchen equipment. This doesn't mean that you have to go out and spend a fortune on expensive gadgets and machinery, but it does make sense to set aside some time to undertake a kitchen cupboard inventory. Once you have an idea of all the equipment you do have, it will be easier to create a shopping list of the things you need to buy.

The following is a comprehensive list of everything you will need to work through all the skills and techniques in this book. However, you won't need everything on the list; you should concentrate on the equipment and utensils that you are likely to use the most. For example, if you are planning to cook lots of fish and shellfish recipes, you might consider buying an oyster shucker and a fish kettle. However, if baking is your main interest, it will be cake pans, scales, and measuring cups that will be at the top of your shopping list.

KNIVES

Chef's or cook's knife
This will be the largest knife in your set. It is multi-purpose and very useful so you should choose a knife that feels comfortable in your hand and is heavier at the base of the blade.

Filleting knife
This has a flexible blade that makes it ideal for preparing fish (e.g., removing fillets).

Boning knife
This is flexible and has a fine tip, which makes it ideal for removing bones and preparing joints and poultry.

Serrated knife
This knife ensures a clean cut and should be used to cut soft-skinned fruit and vegetables, as well as breads and cakes.

Small paring or fruit knife
A smaller version of the chef's knife, this is ideal for neat, precise knife work, such as preparing garlic and chilies, and other detailed cutting.

Carving knife and fork
These are essential when carving cooked meats.

Knife sharpener
These are available in several shapes, such as flat or round. You should experiment to find the one you feel most confident with. It is important to keep knives sharp, as blunt knives are much more dangerous to work with.

KITCHEN UTENSILS

Measuring spoons
These should be bought as a set and are used in many baking recipes.

Measuring cups
Essential for any kitchen and for recipes involving sugar, flour, butter, etc.

Measuring jugs
Choose jugs that are marked with metric and imperial as well as being heatproof and safe for the microwave. It makes sense to have more than one measuring jug.

Scales
You can choose between electronic or balance scales. Electronic is a good choice for baking, as you can usually reset the counter in between ingredients so everything can be added to one mixing bowl.

Timers
Great for keeping organized and remembering that there is something in the oven.

Thermometer
This will come in handy if you intend to do a lot of meat cooking or to work with sugar.

Kitchen shears and poultry shears
It makes sense to have a set of kitchen shears tucked away in a drawer and only used for food. Shears are used for preparing meat and fish.

Vegetable peeler
There are hundreds of designs on the market – choose one that you are most comfortable with. The swivel design tends to work best for all kinds of peeling.

Cutting boards
Choose between wooden or plastic. You can buy color-coded plastic boards for each food group. Be sure to always clean cutting boards thoroughly.

Tongs
You will use these for everything from flipping steaks to serving spaghetti – a must have.

Ladles
Choose a selection of sizes for different dishes.

Spoons
Slotted spoons are required for lifting food from sauces or cooking liquids; whole spoons should be wide and flat and these are used for serving; wooden spoons are indispensable for stirring and are available in a number of sizes.

Zester

If you plan to prepare recipes with citrus zest then this handy little tool should be in your utensil drawer.

Microplane

Always store this with the sheath on and use for shaving thin slices of fruit or vegetables.

Grater

You can choose between a large hollow box shape with four different grating sizes, or specific single sizes – for example, for Parmesan or nutmeg.

Mouli-legumes

A useful tool if you want really smooth mash or vegetable purées.

Palette knife

This flexible utensil is available in a selection of sizes and is essential for baking.

Spatulas

Useful for all different styles of cooking, these are usually rubber and are available in a selection of sizes.

Strainers

You should have a fine strainer for baking and straining stocks and sauces, and a large strainer for draining rice, pasta and other cooked food.

Other utensils

- Apple corer
- Lemon squeezer (glass or plastic)
- Potato masher
- Potato ricer
- Cake slicer

POTS AND PANS

Frying pan

Choose a pan that is low and wide, and ideally heavy based. Have at least two frying pans of different sizes – including one that is nonstick.

Cast iron skillet

This is not essential for everyday cooking but is good for heavy-duty frying.

Pots (with lids)

Choose heavy-based pots in a selection of shapes and sizes for different recipes, e.g., a selection of tall and deep, and low and wide.

Double boiler/steamer

This fits into a low pot and is used for cooking many different ingredients.

Griddle

Choose a cast iron griddle that is heavy. A ridged griddle is best, particularly if you intend to use it to cook steak or fish.

Fish kettle

If seafood is a dinnertime favorite, it is well worth investing in a fish kettle.

Wok

This is essential for stir-fries and is also good for dumplings and other fried recipes.

OVENWARE

Heavy ovenproof casserole dishes with lids

Essential for all everyday cooking as they can be used on the stove too, or first used on the stove and then transferred to the oven.

- Soufflé dishes
- Ramekins – selection of sizes
- Gratin dishes – wide and shallow, best in ceramic

- Roasting pans and trays – selection of sizes and depths
- Racks

BAKEWARE

- Cake pans – round and square, removable bases are ideal
- Spring form cake pans – ideal cake baking pans
- Jelly roll pan – shallow, rectangular
- Cookie sheets – thin, ideally heavy
- Loaf pans
- Pie pans
- Tart pans – fluted edges, removable bases
- Pastry weights – silicone, metal or ceramic

- Tartlet tins – miniature; various shapes
- Cupcake/muffin pans
- Cooling racks
- Pastry cutters – various shapes and sizes
- Silicone molds – various shapes and sizes

- Mixing bowls – glass and stainless steel are ideal
- Pastry brush

- Pestle and mortar – the heavier the better
- Rolling pin

- Whisks – choose various sizes for different uses
- Pastry bags and tips

KITCHEN GADGETS AND MACHINES

- Pasta machine
- Food processor

- Mixer – hand-held and free-standing

- Blender
- Ice cream machine
- Spice grinder
- Deep fat fryer

SAUCE SKILLS

Sauces are the backbone of classic cooking, so once you have mastered some basic recipes your culinary repertoire will expand enormously.

Sauces can often seem daunting and perhaps a little technical – the classic French names themselves can make simple sauces sound far more complicated than they are in reality. But most are easily conquered. Precision and patience are key when tackling sauces such as mayonnaise or béchamel, and it is definitely a case of practice makes perfect. Classic sauces often cannot be rushed; they require time and concentration in order to achieve the best results.

This chapter aims to arm any cook with the tips, skills and confidence to make the perfect hollandaise and endless quantities of glorious gravy. It is worth spending time acquainting yourself with these classic sauce recipes. Once you have learned a few, your kitchen confidence will take a massive leap forward and you will have the skills to make many more recipes and dishes.

1 TOMATO SAUCE

From pasta sauces to pizza toppings, a classic tomato sauce should be in every cook's repertoire.

There are many variations on the classic tomato sauce and once you have mastered this recipe, you can add your own twists and flavors to suit personal preferences, or to work with a specific recipe. For example, a little freshly chopped chili will add heat to your sauce, while chopped anchovies, olives or capers will add extra flavor and texture.

This recipe requires the ingredients to be gently sweated, which means cooking slowly over a low heat, to ensure all the flavor is concentrated in the sauce and the liquid doesn't evaporate. The idea is to soften the onions but not to cook them to the point of browning.

TOOLS AND INGREDIENTS

Sharp chef's knife
Large pot
Wooden spoon or spatula
Fine strainer or food mill
1 tbsp (15 ml) olive oil
1 onion

1 carrot
2 garlic cloves
4–5 large tomatoes
Pinch of sugar
Salt and black pepper

METHOD

1. Heat 1 tablespoon (15 ml) olive oil in a large pot over a low heat.

2. Sweat (see page 53) 1 finely diced onion, 1 finely diced carrot and 2 finely diced garlic cloves for a couple of minutes, until the vegetables have started to soften.

3. Add 4–5 diced fresh tomatoes, with a pinch of sugar, salt and pepper and cook until the vegetables are all soft, about 15–20 minutes.

EXPERT TIPS

* You can use the sauce immediately as a base for spaghetti Bolognese, lasagna or other pasta sauces, or you can let the sauce cool and freeze in batches.

* Always use really fresh, flavorsome tomatoes — they are the main ingredient in the sauce.

* Tomato skin can be bitter so it is best to peel the tomatoes before using (see page 44).

* Try adding chopped fresh herbs such as basil or oregano — stir them into the finished sauce to preserve their flavor and color.

4. Remove the pot from the heat and taste for seasoning, adding more salt, pepper or sugar if needed. Spoon the mix into a fine strainer.

5. Using the back of a spoon, push the sauce through the fine strainer into a large bowl. Alternatively, you can use a food mill.

2 VINAIGRETTE

Vinaigrette is easy to make and can be easily adapted with the addition of extra ingredients. This is a staple salad dressing that all cooks should have up their sleeve.

TOOLS AND INGREDIENTS

Large bowl
Whisk
Screw-top jar (optional)
2 tbsp (30 ml) red or
   white wine vinegar

1 tsp (5 ml) Dijon mustard
Salt and cracked black
   pepper
6 tbsp (90 ml) olive oil

METHOD

1 Put 2 tablespoons (30 ml) red or white wine vinegar, 1 teaspoon (5 ml) Dijon mustard, salt and black pepper into a bowl. Whisk until combined, using a large balloon whisk.

2 Slowly add 6 tablespoons (90 ml) olive oil, whisking constantly, until the vinaigrette has thickened and is smooth.

3 Alternatively, put all the ingredients into a screw-top jar, seal tightly and shake until everything is well combined and thickened.

EXPERT TIPS

* Screw-top jars or other bottles with lids are ideal for making all kinds of uncooked sauces and salad dressings. The key is to screw the lid on tightly and shake vigorously. You can also store the dressing in the jar in the refrigerator.

* You can vary the vinaigrette by adding some freshly diced or dried herbs.

* Always use good quality olive oil, preferably virgin olive oil, and wine vinegar for vinaigrette.

3 GRAVY

From cubes to packets and packages, there are plenty of options for ready-made gravy available in the grocery store. However, good homemade gravy adds another dimension to a roast dinner and the superior flavor makes it well worth the effort.

TOOLS AND INGREDIENTS

Roasting pan
Wooden spoon
Whisk
Fine strainer
Cooking juices

2 tbsp (30 ml) flour
Hot broth
Red or white wine
  (optional)
Salt and black pepper

EXPERT TIPS

* Adding 1 tablespoon (15 ml) red currant or cranberry sauce can be a delicious addition to gravy to be served with lamb. Try using apple juice or cider in a gravy for pork dishes.

* For a rich, creamy flavor, stir in a knob of butter or 1 tablespoon (15 ml) heavy cream just before serving.

METHOD

1. Remove the cooked joint of meat or bird from the roasting pan and set aside to rest.

2. Place the roasting pan on the stove over a medium-low heat and add 2 tablespoons (30 ml) flour. Stir the flour into the cooking juices, making sure you scrape all around the edges to incorporate all of the flavor. Do this until you have a paste, adding more flour if needed.

3. Gradually whisk in a combination of either hot meat or vegetable broth with white or red wine, until you have the desired quantity and consistency.

4. Simmer the gravy on the stove for several minutes and season to taste.

5. Strain the gravy through a fine strainer into a gravy boat to remove the cooking residue so you are left with a silky smooth sauce.

4 MAYONNAISE (BY HAND)

Nothing beats the rich, creamy flavor of homemade mayonnaise. Use for sandwiches, potato salads and as a dip for fries.

TOOLS AND INGREDIENTS

Deep glass bowl
Damp cloth
Whisk
Jug
1 egg yolk
1 tbsp (15 ml) Dijon
  mustard

Salt and pepper
5 fl oz (150 ml) vegetable
  oil
5 fl oz (150 ml) olive oil
1 tsp (5 ml) red or white
  wine vinegar

EXPERT TIPS

* For the best results the ingredients should be at room temperature.

* By using just the egg yolk, the mayonnaise will be richer and thicker in consistency.

METHOD

1. Put a deep glass bowl on a damp cloth to prevent it from slipping.

2. Add 1 egg yolk with 1 tablespoon (15 ml) of Dijon mustard, and salt and pepper, and whisk until the mixture is well combined.

3. Combine 5 fl oz (150 ml) vegetable oil and 5 fl oz (150 ml) olive oil in a jug. Combine this with the egg mixture, working very slowly so the mayonnaise doesn't curdle. Begin by adding the oil drop by drop, whisking constantly. As the oil takes, begin pouring it in a thin steady stream, until it is completely emulsified and thickened.

4. Gradually add 1 teaspoon (5 ml) red or white wine vinegar, whisking constantly, until it is well combined. Season to taste.

5 MAYONNAISE (BY MACHINE)

If time is of the essence, you can let the food processor do all the hard work. As with mayonnaise made by hand, all the ingredients should be at room temperature before you begin.

TOOLS AND INGREDIENTS

Food processor
1 egg
1 tbsp (15 ml) Dijon
 mustard
5 fl oz (150 ml) olive oil

1 tsp (5 ml) red or white
 wine vinegar
Salt and black pepper
5 fl oz (150 ml)
 vegetable oil

EXPERT TIPS

* Use a low setting on the food processor to allow the ingredients to combine well and the mayonnaise to emulsify (the combination of two ingredients that don't naturally mix together – in this case oil and eggs).

* The basic mayonnaise recipe can be adapted with the addition of garlic, chopped herbs or spices.

METHOD

1. Put 1 whole egg and 1 tablespoon (15 ml) Dijon mustard into a food processor and mix until well blended.

2. With the machine running, slowly add 5 fl oz (150 ml) olive oil in a thin, steady stream.

3. Once it has started to thicken, add 1 teaspoon (5 ml) red or white wine vinegar, salt and pepper, and mix until well blended.

4. With the machine running, add 5 fl oz (150 ml) vegetable oil, increasing the flow as the mayonnaise becomes pale. Keep the machine running until the mayonnaise reaches the required consistency. Switch off, season to taste, adding more if required.

VARIATIONS

1. Aïoli (garlic mayonnaise): Replace the Dijon mustard with 4 crushed garlic cloves and ½ teaspoon (3 ml) salt.

2. Herb: Stir in 1 teaspoon (5 ml) each finely chopped parsley, tarragon, chives and chervil to the finished mayonnaise.

6 FIXING MAYONNAISE

Mayonnaise can be temperamental and it might take a few attempts to achieve perfect results. However, if it separates, there are a few tips you can try that might save your mayonnaise. If these don't work, it's best to write off the disaster and start again.

FIXING BY HAND

1. If the mayonnaise splits or curdles, mix 1 tablespoon (15 ml) of cold water or white wine vinegar with 3 tablespoons of the mayonnaise in a separate bowl. Gradually whisk in the remaining mayonnaise and the ingredients should blend together.

FIXING BY MACHINE

1. If the mayonnaise splits or curdles, switch off the food processor and add 1 egg yolk to the mixture. Using the pulse button, mix until the mayonnaise re-emulsifies.

7 HOLLANDAISE

If you can master a perfect hollandaise, you are well on your way to becoming a skilled chef. This go-to sauce is a natural partner for poached eggs (to make eggs Benedict) and fresh asparagus.

TOOLS AND INGREDIENTS

Large pot
Whisk
3 egg yolks
3 tbsp (45 ml) warm water

¾ cup (1½ sticks or 165 g) clarified butter (see page 27)
Juice of ½ lemon
Salt and white pepper

METHOD (BY HAND)

1. Whisk 3 egg yolks and 3 tablespoons (45 ml) warm water together in a pot over a very low heat, until the mixture reaches a ribbon consistency (see expert tips).

2. Add ¾ cup (1½ sticks or 165 g) lukewarm clarified butter (see page 27) in a slow stream, whisking constantly. Slowly whisk in the juice of half a lemon and season to taste.

METHOD (BY MACHINE)

1. Put 3 egg yolks and 3 tablespoons (45 ml) warm water into a food processor. Mix until well combined.

2. With the machine running, slowly add ¾ cup (1½ sticks or 165 g) of lukewarm clarified butter in a slow, steady stream.

3. Add the juice of half a lemon, salt and white pepper.

EXPERT TIPS

* Ribbon consistency describes a mixture thick enough to be lifted from the pot on the back of a spoon while retaining sufficient liquid to fall back again slowly.

* To stop the sauce from curdling, make it in a heatproof bowl over a double boiler.

8 BÉARNAISE

Béarnaise uses the same technique as hollandaise, so if you have mastered one you should easily be able to adapt your skills to create the other.

TOOLS AND INGREDIENTS

Sharp chef's knife
Small pot
Fine strainer
Whisk
4 black peppercorns
1 large shallot
2 tbsp (30 ml) chopped tarragon

3 tbsp (45 ml) red wine vinegar
3 egg yolks
¾ cup (1½ sticks or 165 g) clarified butter (see opposite)
Salt and white pepper

EXPERT TIPS

* This recipe requires patience – whisk the ingredients constantly and never let the temperature get too high or the sauce will curdle (separate).

METHOD

1. Finely chop 1 shallot and place in a small pot with 4 black peppercorns, 2 tablespoons (30 ml) chopped tarragon and 3 tablespoons (45 ml) red wine vinegar.

2. Simmer gently until the vinegar is reduced to about 1 tablespoon (15 ml). Strain the mixture through a fine strainer and return to the pot.

3. Whisk 3 egg yolks and mix into the vinegar over a very low heat, until you have a ribbon consistency (see expert tips page 25).

4. Slowly whisk in ¾ cup (1½ sticks or 165 g) of clarified butter (see opposite) in a slow, steady stream and whisk until the sauce is thickened. Season with salt and white pepper.

9 CLARIFIED BUTTER

Clarified butter is used as an ingredient in a number of recipes (such as hollandaise, page 24 and Béarnaise, page 26) so it is a good skill to add to your repertoire. The process basically involves removing the water and milk solids from the butter in order to leave the fat.

TOOLS AND INGREDIENTS

Small pot
Spoon, for skimming
Storage pot

1 cup (2 sticks or 220 g) butter

METHOD

1. Melt 1 cup (2 sticks or 220 g) of butter in a small pot over very low heat, without stirring.

2. Remove the pot from the heat and use a large spoon to skim the foam off the surface – you will be left with a clear yellow liquid sitting over a milky layer.

3. Spoon the yellow liquid into a container. Discard the milky residue that is left behind.

EXPERT TIPS

* If stored in a sealed, air-tight container, clarified butter will keep in the refrigerator for 2–3 weeks.

10 ROUX

A roux is a thickener that is made from butter and flour and is used as a base ingredient for classic sauces such as béchamel.

TOOLS AND INGREDIENTS

Small pot
Wooden spoon
1 tbsp (15 ml) butter
2 tbsp (30 ml) flour

METHOD

1. Melt 1 tablespoon (15 ml) butter in a small pot and stir in 2 tablespoons (30 ml) flour. Combine until the mixture has a crumbly texture, then cook over a medium heat for approximately 1–2 minutes, until you have a smooth paste.

EXPERT TIPS

* The roux needs to cook for a couple of minutes to remove the taste of flour from the sauce.

11 WHITE SAUCE

A classic white sauce can be served as an accompaniment to broiled fish or chicken. Once you have mastered this essential recipe, you can create a number of variations – freshly squeezed lemon juice, a bay leaf, chopped parsley or a dash of white wine or white wine vinegar all work well.

EXPERT TIPS

* It is important to achieve a smooth consistency in the roux before you begin adding the milk.

* Add the milk very slowly to begin with, until the paste has loosened and more milk can be absorbed.

* Remove the sauce from the heat as soon as the desired consistency is achieved; it will continue to reduce and thicken if left on the heat.

TOOLS AND INGREDIENTS

Medium pot
Whisk
1 tbsp (15 ml) butter

2 tbsp (30 ml) flour
10 fl oz (300 ml) warm milk

METHOD

1. Melt 1 tablespoon (15 ml) butter in a pot and add 2 tablespoons (30 ml) flour. Stir until crumbly then cook over a low heat for 1–2 minutes until you have a thick paste. (This is a roux: see page 27).

2. Remove the pot from the heat and slowly whisk in 10 fl oz (300 ml) warm milk, stirring constantly, until you have a smooth consistency that is free of lumps.

3. Return the pot to a medium-low heat and stir constantly to reduce the consistency of the sauce, until you reach your desired thickness.

12 INFUSING MILK

Heating milk with a selection of aromatic herbs will deepen the flavor of your sauces. For dessert sauces, the milk (or cream) can be infused with vanilla or citrus peel.

TOOLS AND INGREDIENTS

Small pot	6 cloves
Fine strainer	1 bay leaf
10 fl oz (300 ml) milk	Pinch of ground nutmeg
1 small onion	Salt and black pepper

METHOD

1. Place 10 fl oz (300 ml) milk into a small pot and add 1 small onion studded with 6 cloves, 1 bay leaf, ground nutmeg, salt and pepper.

2. Bring to a steady simmer then remove from the heat. Let stand for 10–15 minutes to allow the flavors to infuse. Place a plate on top to keep the onion and herbs submerged.

3. Strain the milk through a fine strainer and discard the flavorings.

13 BÉCHAMEL SAUCE

Béchamel is a traditional French white sauce with a roux base. However, it is usually made with infused milk (see recipe above) to add delicate flavors to the finished sauce. It is used in dishes such as lasagna, croque monsieur and moussaka and is the base for mornay sauce.

METHOD

1. Follow the recipe for White Sauce (opposite) but instead of 10 fl oz (300 ml) warm milk, substitute 10 fl oz (300 ml) infused milk (see recipe above).

14 CRÈME ANGLAISE

This is a classic, sweet French sauce that is a lighter version of the thicker English custard.

TOOLS AND INGREDIENTS

Medium pot x 2
Whisk
Mixing bowl
Wooden spoon

2 cups (500 ml) milk
1 vanilla bean
5 egg yolks
5 tbsp (65 g) superfine sugar

EXPERT TIPS

* If the custard curdles (separates), remove the pot from the heat and beat the mixture until it is smooth.

METHOD

1. Pour 2 cups (500 ml) milk into a small pot and add 1 vanilla bean.

2. Bring to a steady simmer then remove the pot from the heat. Let stand for a few minutes to allow the vanilla to infuse the milk.

3. Meanwhile, whisk 5 egg yolks with 5 tablespoons (65 g) superfine sugar in the bowl, until the mixture is thick and creamy.

4. Remove the vanilla bean from the milk.

5. Whisk the milk into the egg mixture and pour into a clean pot.

6. Heat the crème anglaise gently over a low heat, stirring constantly.

7. Test the consistency by dipping a wooden spoon into the sauce and running your finger across the back of the spoon. It should hold a clear line.

15 CRÈME PATISSIERE

This is another essential sauce in the classic French repertoire. It is a versatile, thick vanilla cream that can be used for cake fillings, fruit tarts or cream puffs.

TOOLS AND INGREDIENTS

Whisk
Mixing bowl
Small pot x 2
Wooden spoon
6 egg yolks

1 cup (225 g) superfine
 sugar
6 tbsp (40 g) cornstarch
6 tbsp (40 g) all-
 purpose flour
2½ cups (600 ml) milk

EXPERT TIPS

* If you are not using the crème patissiere immediately, pour it into a large bowl and lay plastic wrap over the surface so that a skin doesn't form on top of the sauce.

* Allow the crème patissiere to cool before using it in pastry recipes.

METHOD

1. Whisk 6 egg yolks in a bowl, then whisk in 1 cup (225 g) superfine sugar until the mixture becomes thicker and light in color.

2. Whisk in 6 tablespoons (40 g) each of cornstarch and all-purpose flour.

3. Bring 2½ cups (600 ml) milk to a boil in a small pot and stir into the egg mix.

4. Pour the mixture into a clean pot and slowly bring to a boil. Lower the heat and cook gently, stirring constantly, until very thick.

16 SUGAR SYRUP

A handy sweet syrup that is simple to make and can be used in drinks and desserts.

TOOLS AND INGREDIENTS

Heavy pot
Wooden spoon

¾ cup (175 g) white
   sugar
6 fl oz (175 ml) cold water

METHOD

1. Put ¾ cup (175 g) sugar and 6 fl oz (175 ml) cold water in a heavy pot and heat over a low heat.

2. Stir constantly until the sugar has completely dissolved.

3. Boil for 1 minute then remove the pot from the heat and allow the syrup to cool.

EXPERT TIPS

* Sugar syrup will keep in the refrigerator for up to 1 week, in a sealed container.

17 CARAMEL

An essential ingredient in many sweet sauces – or mix with nuts, leave to harden and then process to make praline powder.

TOOLS AND INGREDIENTS

Heavy pot
1 x quantity sugar syrup
  (see recipe left)

METHOD

1. Bring the sugar syrup (see adjacent recipe) to a boil in a heavy pot. Do not stir the syrup.

2. Once it is a deep chestnut brown color, remove from the heat immediately.

3. Put the base of the pot into cold water to prevent the caramel from cooking any further.

EXPERT TIPS

* Caramel expands when it cooks, so use a bigger pot than you think you might need to help to protect you from the boiling sugar.

* If the caramel burns, remove it from the pot immediately — once set, it is difficult to dislodge. To clean the pot, cover the caramel residue with water and heat until it melts, then scrub in hot soapy water.

18 CHOCOLATE SAUCE (GANACHE)

Chocolate sauce is an essential recipe to have at your fingertips – from cake fillings to fruit kabobs, coated cookies to dessert topplngs, the list of uses is endless. This is a very simple recipe that involves the careful heating and mixing of two indulgent ingredients.

METHOD

1. Heat 5 fl oz (150 ml) of heavy cream in a pot until just below boiling point then remove from the heat.

2. Dice 11 ounces (325 g) good-quality semi-sweet chocolate into small pieces and stir into the hot cream. Keep stirring until the chocolate has completely melted, then let the sauce cool (or serve warm over desserts).

EXPERT TIPS

* Always choose good-quality chocolate with a high cocoa butter content, and allow it come to room temperature so it is easier to cut.

* If you prefer, you can melt the chocolate in the heatproof bowl of a double boiler. Once melted, slowly pour the hot cream over the chocolate and stir constantly to combine. Let cool before using.

* Chocolate sauce can be used to decorate cakes: let cool completely, then spoon it into a pastry bag.

TOOLS AND INGREDIENTS

Medium pot
Sharp chef's knife
Cutting board
5 fl oz (150 ml) heavy
  cream

11 oz (325 g) semisweet
  chocolate

VEGETABLE SKILLS

There is more to vegetable preparation than slicing carrots and bringing a pot of water to a boil. If you learn to peel, dice, purée, char, glaze and caramelize properly, you will save yourself a lot of time and effort.

This chapter will introduce you to the essential skills for preparing all kinds of vegetables in many different ways – from peeling and pitting an avocado, to creating the perfect julienne – so you will feel more confident when it comes to the skills required for recipes.

These days, vegetables are no longer an afterthought, a sad little garnish on the side of a plate of meat. They are often the stars of the show, which makes it all the more important to learn how to prepare and cook them properly.

19 DICING AN ONION

Onions are staple ingredients in so many recipes that it makes sense to master the skill of preparing them first. This is a neat, precise slicing method that ensures all the pieces of the onion cook evenly in the pot.

TOOLS AND INGREDIENTS

Sharp chef's knife
Cutting board
1 onion

METHOD

1 First peel the onion by cutting it in half lengthwise then peeling back the skin of each half to the root. Don't cut off the root – leave it in place, as this makes it easier to cut the onion. Cut the tip off each onion half.

2 Working with one onion half at a time, put it flat side-down on a cutting board. Slice along the onion 2–3 times lengthwise through to the cutting board but not slicing to the end of the root – keep this intact and use it to hold the onion in place.

3 Now cut widthwise down the onion in regular slices, but again not cutting all the way to the root.

4 Cut across the onion evenly, up to the root, to get a neat dice.

EXPERT TIPS

* If you need very small pieces for a recipe, or you are dicing onions to make a sauce, you can use a coarse grater. Peel and cut the onion in half, then carefully shred each half.

20 SLICING AN ONION

Slicing is a master method that can be applied to almost all vegetables. A large chef's knife that is sharp is essential. Again, it is important to cut even-sized slices so that all the pieces cook evenly. You can create thicker or thinner slices, depending on the recipe – a chunky sauce might require thicker slices, while a salad will call for thinner, more delicate slices.

TOOLS AND INGREDIENTS

Sharp chef's knife
Cutting board
1 onion

METHOD

1 First peel the onion by cutting it in half lengthwise then peeling back the skin of each half to the root. Don't cut off the root – leave it in place, as this makes it easier to cut the onion. Cut the tip off each onion half.

2 Working with one onion half at a time, place it flat side-down on a cutting board. Slice the onion at even intervals, at the required width, working from the tip to the root. Finally, cut off the root to leave neat slices.

EXPERT TIPS

* An alternative is to slice the onion on a mandolin (vegetable slicer). Peel the onion, cut it in half and set the mandolin to the required width. This technique will result in very uniform slices.

* When cutting onions, keep the exposed part of the onion facing away from you – this will cut down on the amount of vapor going into your eyes.

21 PEELING GARLIC

Garlic is another staple in the cook's cupboard. Although there are quick alternatives for busy chefs, nothing beats freshly prepared garlic cloves, so it's worth spending the extra time mastering garlic preparation for a more authentic flavor in your recipes.

TOOLS AND INGREDIENTS

Cutting board
Large chef's knife

Garlic cloves (according
to recipe)

METHOD

1. Separate the number of individual cloves that you need from the bulb.

2. Put a garlic clove on a cutting board and cover with the flat side of a large chef's knife.

3. Press down firmly on the knife with your fist, making sure the clove stays in place underneath. It should feel like you are squashing the garlic but not completely flattening it.

4. Remove the knife and the garlic skin should be loosened so that you can peel it away easily with your fingers.

38

④

22 MINCING GARLIC

This simple skill produces a very fine dice, which means the garlic can be used in recipes for salad dressings, sauces and salads without the tangy bite that larger pieces of garlic produce.

TOOLS AND INGREDIENTS

Cutting board
Sharp chef's knife

Garlic cloves (according
to recipe)

METHOD

1. Peel the number of garlic cloves you require (see adjacent skill) and put on a cutting board.

2. Keep each clove steady with one hand and use a sharp chef's knife to slice the cloves thinly, in even strips.

3. Alternatively, you can cut each clove of garlic in half and roughly chop each half.

4. Gather all the chopped garlic in the center of the board and run the knife backward and forward in a rocking motion until the garlic is very finely diced.

④

23 CREAMING GARLIC

Creaming garlic to get a smooth paste is a quick way to add depth of flavor to many dishes. It is ideal for using in soups, sauces and stews, as the flavor is present without the bite of whole chunks of garlic.

TOOLS AND INGREDIENTS

Cutting board
Sharp chef's knife

Garlic cloves (according to recipe)
Salt

EXPERT TIPS

* An alternative method is to shred the garlic with a fine grater and then rub in the salt to create a paste.

* Creamed garlic is used in aïoli (garlic mayonnaise). Simply make a fresh batch of mayonnaise (see page 22) and stir in the creamed garlic at the end.

METHOD

1. Peel the number of garlic cloves you require (see opposite page) and crush the garlic on a cutting board, using the flat side of a large chef's knife and pressing down firmly.

2. Sprinkle the garlic with a pinch of salt and roughly slice up the cloves.

3. Again, using the flat side of a sharp chef's knife, rub the garlic across the cutting board to combine it with the salt. This will produce a smooth paste.

24 ALLUMETTE

This skill, cutting into matchstick-size pieces, is ideal for potatoes or other root vegetables.

TOOLS AND INGREDIENTS

Sharp chef's knife
Cutting board
Large potatoes

METHOD (USING POTATO)

1. Wash and peel the potatoes. Cut each potato in half lengthwise and trim off the ends and sides to create even, rectangular shapes.

2. Cut each potato half into thin slices, about ¼ inch (5 mm) wide.

3. Lay the potato slices flat on the cutting board and cut them into thin matchsticks, ¼ inch (5 mm) wide.

25 BATONNET

This is a smart, uniform slice that works well for crudités and vegetable accompaniments where presentation is important.

TOOLS AND INGREDIENTS

Sharp chef's knife
Cutting board
Carrots

METHOD (USING CARROT)

1. Peel a carrot and cut it in half across the width and then the length, taking care to cut the pieces into even sizes.

2. Slice each carrot half into 2 or 3 slices lengthwise, about ½ inch (1 cm) thick.

3. Lay the slices flat on the cutting board and cut each slice into batons 2 inches (5 cm) long.

26 BRUNOISE

This knife skill produces a very fine dice, so it requires precision cutting and a steady hand.

TOOLS AND INGREDIENTS

Sharp chef's knife
Cutting board
Leeks

METHOD (USING LEEK)

1. Clean and trim the leeks, making sure you remove any grit that is lying inside the inner layers.

2. Slice each leek lengthwise into very thin, even strips.

3. Working slowly along the leeks, cut down to create a fine, even dice.

27 CHIFFONADE

This simple knife technique is used on leaves or herbs. Green vegetables such as cabbage will soften and cook quickly when cut using this technique, without going soggy.

TOOLS AND INGREDIENTS

Sharp chef's knife   Cabbage
Cutting board

METHOD (USING CABBAGE)

1. Remove the tough core and stalks from the cabbage leaves. Also remove any tough outer leaves.

2. Stack all the leaves on top of each other, then loosely roll them up into a cylinder.

3. Slice finely across the roll to create a pile of evenly shredded leaves.

28 JULIENNE

This is a French-named skill that is used to slice vegetables into very fine strips. The delicate slices are perfect for using as garnishes, either presented raw or deep-fried for a crispy texture.

METHOD (USING LEEK)

1. Wash and trim the leeks, ensuring all the grit has been removed from the inner layers.

2. Remove the darker and tougher outer green leaves, leaving the white, central part of the leeks. Using a sharp knife carefully cut each leek in half lengthwise from end to end. If the leeks are long, cut them in half crosswise — or make a number of cuts, depending on the length of "julienne" you require.

3. Put the halved leeks flat side-down on the cutting board and cut lengthwise into very fine strips that are all equal width.

TOOLS AND INGREDIENTS

Sharp chef's knife
Cutting board
Leeks

EXPERT TIPS

* Once you have made the julienne, put the vegetables into a bowl of ice water until you are ready to use them — this will prevent them from wilting or discoloring.

29 SHREDDING

This is a useful knife skill for leafy vegetables such as cabbage. It is simple to master – the important thing is to work with a very sharp knife so the vegetables are sliced neatly, rather than being torn with a blunt knife.

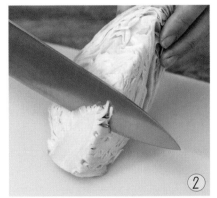

TOOLS AND INGREDIENTS

Sharp chef's knife
Cutting board
Savoy cabbage

METHOD (USING CABBAGE)

1. Remove the tough outer leaves of a savoy cabbage.

2. Separate the leaves and cut out the tough core from each leaf. You can do this by slicing a "V" shape into the leaf at the base, using a sharp knife.

3. Neatly lay the leaves on top of each other.

EXPERT TIPS

* Try this technique with herbs such as basil and parsley but use the herbs immediately after cutting or they will begin to wilt.

4. Cut across the leaves evenly and finely, creating thin strips.

5. Cut the remaining inner part of the cabbage into quarters. Cut finely across each piece for evenly shredded leaves.

6. Put the shredded cabbage into a bowl of water to keep it fresh and vibrant, until you need to use it.

30 PEELING TOMATOES

Tomatoes are essential ingredients in numerous recipes so it makes sense to master the skills of preparing them quickly, neatly and efficiently.

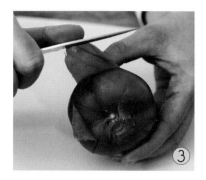

TOOLS AND INGREDIENTS

Sharp chef's knife
Heatproof bowl
Paring knife

Cutting board
Tomatoes (according to recipe)

EXPERT TIPS

* Tomato skin can have a bitter taste so it is worth the effort of peeling them for delicate sauces or when using as a garnish – for example, to accompany gazpacho.

* The tomatoes will be very hot when they come out of the bowl so you might need to wait a few seconds before handling them – if you can't wait, use a clean dish towel to hold them while you peel off the skins.

METHOD

1. Using a sharp chef's knife, lightly score the tomatoes by marking a cross over the top of each one.

2. Put the tomatoes in a large, heatproof bowl, cover with boiling water and leave for about 15 seconds.

3. Drain the tomatoes and peel off the skin using a small paring knife. The skins should come away easily, with just a little encouragement from the knife.

4. Slice the tomatoes in half, remove the seeds and the tough core then dice (or as indicated by the recipe).

31 PEELING SHALLOTS

Shallots have a distinctive, sweet flavor but their diminutive size means they are trickier to peel than onions. Recipes often call for a number of shallots so this method will save you time when prepping the ingredients.

METHOD

1. Fill a heatproof bowl with boiling water.

2. Put the shallots in the bowl and leave for about 15 seconds to soften and loosen the skins.

3. Drain the shallots and fill the bowl with cold water. Leave them for about 1 minute – this stops the "cooking" process that would have begun briefly when the shallots were immersed in boiling water.

4. Drain the shallots and peel the skin away using a sharp chef's knife.

TOOLS AND INGREDIENTS

Heatproof bowl
Sharp chef's knife
Shallots (according to
  recipe)

EXPERT TIPS

* If the skins aren't too tough, an alternative method is to remove the ends of each shallot, slice carefully through the skin and simply peel it back, all the way around the shallot – then cut off at the same time as the root.

32 PITTING AVOCADOS

The effort involved in getting into an avocado often seems to outweigh the desire to eat one – these simple techniques will change that.

TOOLS AND INGREDIENTS

Sharp chef's knife
Cutting board
Avocado

METHOD

1 Run a sharp chef's knife lengthwise along the middle of the avocado, around the whole fruit, cutting through to the pit.

2 Hold the avocado in both hands and gently twist the avocado, rotating the halves in opposite directions to separate them.

3. Hold the half with the pit in the palm of one hand, and firmly tap the knife blade into the pit so that it holds firm. Use the knife handle to twist the pit until it loosens and pulls free.

EXPERT TIPS

* Cut avocados discolor quickly — keep them vibrant by squeezing lemon juice over the exposed sections.

* The flesh of a ripe avocado should yield to firm but gentle pressure. To ripen one at home, store at room temperature and check it every 2–3 days.

33 PEELING AVOCADOS

Removing the flesh from the skin is a simple operation with these techniques.

TOOLS AND INGREDIENTS

Sharp chef's knife   Avocado
Cutting board
Tablespoon

METHOD

1. Hold the avocado in one hand.

2. Use a small chef's knife to score the skin, lengthwise, into quarters.

3. Start at one end and use the blade of the knife to peel the skin of one quarter back and down the length of the avocado. Repeat with the other sections.

4. Alternatively, pit the avocado and then scoop out the flesh using a tablespoon.

34 CUTTING CHILIES

Chilies give recipes a delicious kick but if you don't prepare them properly, you might get more fire than you bargained for.

①

②

④

TOOLS AND INGREDIENTS

Sharp chef's knife   Small paring knife
Cutting board   Chili
Small bowl

EXPERT TIPS

* Some chilies are more pungent than others and the juice will burn so avoid touching your eyes and cover any cuts in your skin.

* Some people wear rubber gloves to ensure the chili oil stays away from their hands but this makes knife work a little more cumbersome.

* Alternatively, wash your hands with plenty of warm, soapy water to help loosen and remove the oil.

METHOD

1. Roll the chili between your hands to loosen the seeds (if you wish to cook without them).

2. Slice the whole top off the chili and tap the chili against the side of a small bowl. The seeds should all fall out.

3. Slice the chili in half lengthwise and cut out any white fibers, using a small paring knife (these also contain a lot of heat so removing them will result in a subtler flavor).

4. Either finely slice or dice the chili, depending on the recipe requirements.

35 PREPARING AND SHREDDING GINGER OR FRESH HORSERADISH

Ginger and horseradish are both popular ingredients used to add heat to a dish. However, both are fibrous and can be difficult to slice with a knife. This method ensures the whole piece is used and the ingredient is uniformly shredded.

(1)

(2)

TOOLS AND INGREDIENTS

Small paring knife,
  teaspoon or peeler
Sharp chef's knife
  (optional)

Mandolin or fine grater
Ginger or horseradish

METHOD

1 Using a small paring knife, teaspoon or peeler, scrape the skin off the ginger or horseradish. If the skin is very tough, use a sharp chef's knife to slice down the skin and remove it, working around the piece of ginger or horseradish.

EXPERT TIPS

* Keep fresh ginger or horseradish wrapped in plastic wrap in the freezer, as it is easier to peel and shred when frozen.

* If you want more defined pieces of ginger, you can use the julienne technique (see page 42) to prepare it.

2 Using a mandolin for fine slices, or a fine grater for shreds and purée, run the ginger or horseradish up and down, turning it as you work, so that the fibers are all incorporated.

36 HERBS

Herbs are an essential addition to a chef's kitchen and they can elevate so many recipes. From broths, salads and stews to scrambled eggs, fish dishes and game, the flavor of herbs can add ranges from subtle to pungent.

TOOLS AND INGREDIENTS

Sharp chef's knife
Cutting board
Kitchen shears
Selection of herbs

CHOPPING PARSLEY

1. Strip all the leaves from the stalks.

2. Gather the leaves together into a loose bunch and chop using a sharp chef's knife.

3. You can leave the leaves as roughly chopped, or continue, depending on how finely chopped you want the herbs to be.

* The flavor of fresh herbs is far superior to dried. However, if you have to use dried make sure they are not too old – dried herbs soon taste dull and dusty.

* Many herbs are easy to grow in the garden, in pots on the patio, or the kitchen windowsill. If you plan to do this the ones you may find most useful are mint, basil, sage, chives, parsley, dill, tarragon, thyme and chervil.

* If you want to use fresh herbs from the store they should keep for a few days in a vase or glass of water like cut flowers.

* Herbes de Provence – a mixture of thyme, rosemary, basil, savory and sometimes lavender – is often sold as a dried mixture. Serve with barbecued lamb for a taste of the Mediterranean.

SNIPPING CHIVES

1 Gather the chives together in a neat bunch and hold it fairly tightly in one hand.

2 With the other hand, cut or snip the chives into short pieces, using kitchen shears.

SHREDDING BASIL

1 Pile the basil leaves on top of each other, trying to keep them in a neat pile.

2 Roll up into a cylinder and slice firmly using a chef's knife.

37 BLANCHING

Blanching is the process in which fruit or vegetables are briefly immersed in boiling water then transferred to cold water in order to halt the cooking process. Blanching doesn't so much cook food as pre-cooks or partially cooks it. It is also used to make skinning fruit or vegetables (such as tomatoes or plums, see pages 44 and 66) easier.

TOOLS AND INGREDIENTS

Large pot
Strainer
Salt

Vegetables or fruit
   (according to recipe)

METHOD

1. Bring a large pot of water to a boil; add salt.

2. Once the water has reached a rolling boil, add the prepared vegetables and simmer. The amount of time the vegetables or fruit are left to simmer depends on the recipe. For example, tomatoes will only need 30 seconds or so for the skins to loosen, whereas blanching green beans will take 3–5 minutes.

EXPERT TIPS

* You can blanch vegetables in advance and keep in the refrigerator for a few hours until needed. This can save time if you are preparing a complicated recipe, or need to put something together in a hurry.

* Don't be shy with salt – add about 2 teaspoons (10 ml) to the cooking water.

3. Drain the vegetables in a strainer and immediately plunge them into cold water to refresh, keep the color and prevent any further cooking.

38 SWEATING VEGETABLES

The idea behind this technique is to release moisture from the vegetables so that little fat is needed. The vegetables are cooked gently over a low heat, in order to soften them rather than cook through and brown them. You will often be required to sweat ingredients at the beginning of a recipe, before other ingredients are prepared and cooked.

METHOD

1. Prepare the vegetables (this could be a mirepoix – a combination of onion, carrots and celery, or a single vegetable such as onions or leeks) by dicing them (see page 36) so that they are all of a uniform size and cook at the same time.

2. Heat 2 tablespoons (30 ml) butter in a wide pot, add the vegetables and sprinkle with salt and pepper.

3. Cover with a parchment paper cartouche (see page 63).

4. Cook the vegetables gently over a low heat for about 5 minutes, until they are beginning to soften, but do not let them color. Stir constantly so the vegetables cook evenly.

TOOLS AND INGREDIENTS

Wide pot
Sharp chef's knife
Parchment paper
 cartouche (see page 63)

2 tbsp (30 ml) butter
Vegetables (according to
 recipe)
Salt and black pepper

EXPERT TIPS

* The addition of salt helps to release the moisture from the vegetables.

39 GLAZING VEGETABLES

Glazed vegetables shine brightly with a coating that is part glaze, part sauce. This is a lovely technique for giving the humble root vegetable more of a starring role on the dinner plate. The flavor is richer and sweeter, too. The choice of vegetables is up to you (or dependent on the recipe) but carrots and other root vegetables work particularly well.

TOOLS AND INGREDIENTS

Heavy pot
Wooden spoon
2 tbsp (30 ml) butter
Water

Salt
White or superfine sugar
Vegetables (according to
   recipe)

EXPERT TIPS

* Carrots taste better if they retain a little bite. However, other root vegetables such as parsnips might need a longer cooking time or to be cut into smaller pieces.

* If there is any glaze left in the pot, drizzle this over the vegetables just before serving.

METHOD

1. Blanch the vegetables in boiling water (see page 52). You can do this a few hours in advance or just before you need them.

2. In a heavy pot, melt 2 tablespoons (30 ml) butter. Add the vegetables, enough water to half cover them, and a pinch of salt and sugar.

3. Cook the vegetables over a high heat, stirring frequently for about 5 minutes or until the liquid has reduced to a thick glaze and the vegetables are tender.

40 PURÉEING AND MASHING

A purée has a more liquid consistency than a mash but essentially the same technique is used to create creamy vegetables.

TOOLS AND INGREDIENTS

Large pot
Food mill or tamis (drum
  strainer)
Large bowl
Serving spoon or plastic
  scraper
Potatoes (quantity
  according to recipe)

¼ cup (½ stick or 50 g)
  butter
4 tbsp (60 ml) whole milk
  or heavy cream
(These quantities are for
  2 lb/1 kg of potatoes)

METHOD (USING POTATOES)

1. Skin and dice the potatoes into large, uniform pieces. Cook in a large pot of boiling water for about 15–20 minutes or until soft and cooked through.

2. Drain the potatoes thoroughly to remove as much liquid as possible.

3. Place a food mill over a large bowl and put the cooked potatoes in it. Turn the handle until all the potatoes have been passed through into the bowl.

4. Alternatively, put a tamis over a large bowl, and press the potatoes through using a large spoon or plastic scraper.

5. Stir through the butter and mix to combine.

6. If making purée, the consistency needs to be wetter. Add the milk or heavy cream and mix well, adjusting the amounts, until you have achieved the desired consistency.

EXPERT TIPS

* If you use a traditional potato masher purée the potatoes thoroughly so that no lumps remain.

55

41 CHARGRILLING VEGETABLES

Chargrilled vegetables are packed full of rich, smoky flavor and they make a great base for a ratatouille or chunky pasta sauce. Alternatively, serve with steamed couscous and a spoon of tzatziki or pesto.

METHOD

1. Heat a ridged griddle over a very high heat until it is hot.

2. Prepare the vegetables and slice or cut into large pieces as required. Toss in a little olive oil and place on the griddle so that all the pieces are flat and touching the base.

3. Cook for about 5 minutes on each side, or until you have a lined effect from the griddle and the vegetables are cooked but still retain texture and bite.

TOOLS AND INGREDIENTS

Ridged griddle
Tongs
Olive oil
Vegetables (e.g., peppers,
  zucchini, onions,
  eggplant, mushrooms)

EXPERT TIPS

* You can also chargrill vegetables on the barbecue. The same method applies and it is important that all the pieces are coated in oil so they don't stick to the grill.

* Cut the vegetables into thick slices so that they hold their shape during cooking. Brush the vegetables with oil or a marinade during cooking and again when you turn them over.

42 CHARRING AND PEELING PEPPERS

Peppers have a naturally sweet flavor when cooked and charring concentrates this flavor even more. Add slices of charred pepper to salads, purée for soups, or use in sandwiches.

EXPERT TIPS

* You can use a food bag to cool the pepper instead of a heatproof bowl — seal it tightly so the steam doesn't escape.

* Chargrilled peppers also work well on barbecues — you can hold them directly over the charcoal with tongs, or put them on the cooking rack in a hot part of the barbecue.

* If you don't have a gas stove, you can blacken the skins on a broiler.

TOOLS AND INGREDIENTS

Tongs
Heatproof bowl
Plastic wrap

Bell peppers (number and color according to recipe)

METHOD

1. Using tongs, hold the pepper directly over a gas stove flame, turning regularly until it is evenly blackened and charred.

2. Put the pepper immediately into a heatproof bowl and cover it tightly with plastic wrap; leave for a minimum of 15 minutes. This lets the pepper cool down and sweat so that the skin is removed more easily.

3. Use your hands to peel off the skin, which should come off easily, and rinse the pepper under warm running water.

4. Now you can remove the core and seeds and slice the pepper into strips or dice, depending on the recipe.

43 CARAMELIZING ONIONS

Caramelizing releases the natural sweetness of onions and although time consuming – there are no shortcuts – this skill is easy to master and the results speak for themselves.

TOOLS AND INGREDIENTS

Sharp chef's knife
Cutting board
Heavy pot with lid
Wooden spoon or stirrer
Paper cartouche (optional, see page 63)

¼ cup (½ stick or 50 g) butter
2 large onions or 4 large shallots
Salt

METHOD

1. Heat ¼ cup (½ stick or 50 g) butter in a heavy pot with a lid, over a low heat.

2. Finely slice the onions (see page 37) or keep the shallots whole (as required) and add to the pot with a pinch of salt. Stir well until they are coated with butter.

3. Cover the pot (you could use a parchment paper cartouche – see page 63 – first) and cook very slowly, stirring occasionally, for about 40 minutes. You do not want the onions to color too quickly, so reduce the heat if necessary.

4. After 40 minutes the onions should be soft and translucent. Remove the lid and increase the heat, stirring frequently, until they are a dark caramel color with a sticky consistency. This should take a further 15–20 minutes but reduce the heat if they color too quickly.

EXPERT TIPS

* The caramelized onions will store in the refrigerator for up to 3 days in a sealed container.

44 SALTING EGGPLANTS

Eggplants have a slightly bitter flavor and salting them before cooking helps to reduce this. It also prevents the eggplants from absorbing too much oil during cooking and becoming greasy.

METHOD

1. Trim off the stalk and slice the eggplant(s) into even, horizontal slices.

2. Spread the slices in an even layer in a strainer that is put over a large serving plate or bowl.

3. Sprinkle the slices generously with salt all over and let stand for a minimum of 30 minutes.

4. Rinse the slices under cold water and dry well before cooking. You can use paper towels or a clean dish towel to do this.

TOOLS AND INGREDIENTS

Sharp chef's knife
Cutting board
Strainer

Large plate or bowl
Eggplant(s)
Salt

EXPERT TIPS

* Don't scrimp on the salt – it might seem like you are adding a lot, but it is there to draw out the moisture and most will be removed when you rinse the eggplant.

* You can also use this technique for zucchini.

45 BRUISING AND CHOPPING LEMON GRASS

The delicate citrus aroma and flavor of lemon grass gives many Asian dishes their distinctive personality. Although the stalks might look impenetrable, they are relatively easy to work with. Bruising the lemon grass before chopping helps to release the flavor and also to soften the stalks and make them more pliable.

TOOLS AND INGREDIENTS

Sharp chef's knife
Rolling pin (optional)
Cutting board

Lemon grass (according to recipe)

EXPERT TIPS

* When buying lemon grass choose stalks that have a strong aroma and avoid any with brown stems, as these will be dry and will have lost their fresh, vibrant flavor.

* For a more subtle flavor, you can simply bend the lemon grass in a couple of places along the stalks, rather than pounding with a rolling pin.

METHOD

1. Trim away the tough tops and bottoms of the stalks and peel away the outer layer, as this will also be tough.

2. Using the handle of a chef's knife, or a rolling pin, bruise the lemon grass stalks all over by hitting them fairly hard. This tenderizes the lemon grass and releases the aroma and flavor so that it will be more readily absorbed by the other ingredients.

3. Finely chop the lemon grass (if required by the recipe).

46 SOAKING DRIED MUSHROOMS

A dehydrated mushroom isn't much to look at but once it has been soaked in water and regained its shape and moisture, the flavor punch is incredible. Use in risottos, omelets and stir-fries. If you aren't eager to go foraging, or if the price of fresh specialty mushrooms at the store is too high, then dried mushrooms are the next best way to enjoy wild and exotic mushrooms all year round.

TOOLS AND INGREDIENTS

Heatproof bowl
Fine strainer
Dried mushrooms
  (according to recipe)

METHOD

1. Put the dried mushrooms in a small heatproof bowl.

2. Add enough boiling water to cover the mushrooms completely, ensuring that the mushrooms are spread out and have plenty of space to soak up the liquid.

3. Let the mushrooms soak for 10–15 minutes until they are rehydrated. Strain through a fine strainer, reserving the liquid.

4. Be sure to rinse any grit from the mushrooms once more before using.

EXPERT TIPS

* Don't throw the soaking liquid away – it can be used in the same way as a broth for soups or stews, but strain it through cheesecloth or a fine strainer first to remove any grit or sand.

* Dried mushrooms are essential cupboard ingredients: they keep for months and take minutes to prepare.

47 BOUQUET GARNI

A bouquet garni is basically a bundle of herbs that is added whole to soups, stews or other one-pot recipes in order to subtly infuse the dish with extra flavor. The following technique uses the traditional recipe for a bouquet garni, however some recipes may call for different herbs – or you can create your own variations.

TOOLS AND INGREDIENTS

Kitchen twine
Cheesecloth (optional)
1 sprig each thyme,
   rosemary, parsley
1 bay leaf

METHOD

1 Make a neat bouquet by gathering together 1 sprig of thyme, 1 of rosemary, 1 of parsley (flat leaf or curly) and 1 bay leaf. Hold them tightly in one hand and tie together with kitchen twine. Wrap the twine around the garni a couple of times to ensure the herbs stay together in the pot.

2 For easy removal from the cooking pot, you can tie the bouquet garni onto a separate, long piece of kitchen twine and then tie this to the pot handle. Alternatively, wrap the garni in a small square of cheesecloth.

EXPERT TIPS

* Don't forget to remove the bouquet garni from the pot before serving – guests won't appreciate a bundle of twigs and twine on their plate.

* For a more intense flavor, you can finely chop the herbs first, and then place in a square of cheesecloth. Secure it tightly and drop it into the pot.

48 PARCHMENT PAPER CARTOUCHE

A cartouche acts as a cozy hat for a cooking pot – it fits snugly over the food to keep all the moisture in the dish, stopping the food drying out and keeping finished dishes warm. You can also use this technique when cutting paper to line cake or tart pans.

TOOLS AND INGREDIENTS

Parchment paper
Kitchen shears

EXPERT TIPS

* Another way to make a cartouche is to take a large square of parchment paper and lay it flat on the work surface. Place the pot you will be using face-down on the paper and trace around its rim. Now cut out the cartouche and it will fit the pot exactly. (Cut just inside the drawn line to avoid any pencil or pen marks touching the food.)

METHOD

1. Take a large square piece of parchment paper.

2. Neatly fold the paper in half, and then fold it in half again. Now fold in half again, diagonally across the square, to form a triangle.

3. Hold one point above the center of the pot and cut around the flat side so that it matches the edge of the pot.

4. Open out the paper and you should have a circle that fits perfectly inside the pot. Now simply lay this over the food so that it is a snug fit. Some recipes will require a lid on the pot as well; others just call for a cartouche.

FRUIT AND NUT SKILLS

Whether it is part of a recipe, a refreshing finish to a meal or a breakfast fruit salad, fresh fruit is one of life's pleasures. Sweet, juicy, healthy and delicious – and with an almost endless selection of shapes, flavors and colors – fruit should be on the menu at every meal.

When it comes to preparing fruit, it is very important not to cause bruising, so a light touch and the correct utensils and knife skills are vital. Picking fruit that is ripe, in season and of high quality is essential, and it is best to handle the fruit as little as possible.

Nuts add texture to many dishes, or make a delicious snack of their own. Skinning and toasting them can transform their flavor.

This chapter aims to offer the most useful tips for preparing fruit and nuts – from peeling and pitting to baking and poaching.

49 PEELING FRUIT

It might sound simple but it is important to be able to peel fruit so that it doesn't bruise and as little flesh as possible is lost.

TOOLS AND INGREDIENTS

Peeler
Fruit (according to recipe)

METHOD

1. Core the fruit, if necessary (see page 67).

2. Using a peeler (one with a pointed tip, not swivel), peel the skin, starting at the top of the fruit and working downward. Work carefully in order to remove all the skin, while retaining all the flesh underneath.

50 SKINNING FRUIT

With this technique you are aiming to remove a very thin layer of skin from the fruit. It is used for stone fruit such as apricots and peaches.

TOOLS AND INGREDIENTS

Large pot
Bowl

Small paring or fruit knife
Fruit (according to recipe)

METHOD

1. Blanch the fruit (see page 52) in boiling water for 10-20 seconds, depending on ripeness.

2. Immediately transfer the fruit to a bowl of ice-cold water to stop the "cooking" process – leave very briefly and then lift out.

3. Starting from the stalk, peel the skin back with a small paring or fruit knife, working around the fruit until all the skin is removed.

51 CORING FRUIT

There is a skill involved in cleanly removing the core from fruit. If the cut is not neat, you will end up removing the flesh as well. You can use a corer, a pointed tip vegetable peeler, or a melon baller to core fruit – try practicing with each to see which works best for you.

TOOLS AND INGREDIENTS

Corer, vegetable peeler or
 melon baller
Fruit (according to recipe)

EXPERT TIPS

* The flesh of fruit such as apples and pears turns brown once cut. To help to prevent this drop the peeled or sliced fruit into acidulated water – water which has had a little lemon juice added to it.

METHOD

1. If you are using a corer, place it over the stalk or core of the fruit and firmly push it down and through the center of the fruit until you reach the bottom.

2. Rotate the corer gently to loosen the core. When you can feel that the core has come free from the fruit, pull the corer out.

3. If you are using a pointed-tip vegetable peeler, push the pointed tip into the core of the fruit, from the bottom upward.

4. Twist it once inside the fruit and then gently pull it out – the core should be removed easily.

5. If using a melon baller, cut the fruit in half first.

6. Using the baller, scoop out the seeds and heart of the core, leaving a neat finish if the center of the fruit is going to be on display when served.

52 REMOVING PITS

Different varieties of fruit require different amounts of pressure when removing the pit. If the fruit is very ripe, you will need to take extra care because the flesh will be delicate.

 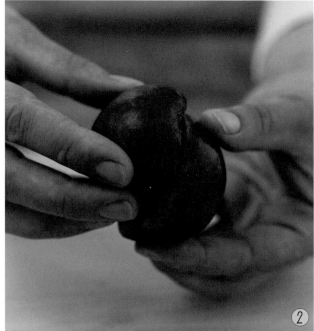

TOOLS AND INGREDIENTS

Small paring or fruit knife
Sharp chef's knife
  (optional)
Fruit (according to recipe)

METHOD

1. Carefully cut around the center of the fruit (this could be plums or peaches, for example) with a small paring knife or fruit knife. Cut right through to the pit and work in an even circle so the cut is one continuous line around the fruit.

2. Gently twist the two halves of the fruit in opposite directions to separate them from the pit. Pull the halves apart and keep the half containing the pit in one hand.

3. If you can't remove the pit with your fingers but the fruit is too small or too soft to use a sharp knife, you can use a teaspoon to loosen the area around the pit.

4. If the fruit is slightly under-ripe, this will be more difficult, in which case you will need to lift the pit out with the tip of the knife. Hold the knife handle firmly and tap the blade of the knife down into the center of the pit. Twist the blade to loosen the pit and then lift out the knife – the pit should come out at the same time.

EXPERT TIPS

* If the fruit is slippery and you find it difficult to get a firm grip, use a clean dish towel to hold it while removing the pit.

* Depending on the ripeness of the fruit, you might be able to work the pit out with your fingers without damaging the flesh.

* Use the cut fruit immediately as the flesh will discolor quickly and start to dry out.

53 PEELING A PINEAPPLE

Canned pineapple has its place but if you're preparing a fruit salad or other dish where the fruit is the star, then fresh is always best.

TOOLS AND INGREDIENTS

Large serrated knife   Pineapple
Cutting board   Cutter or corer
Paring knife or fruit knife

EXPERT TIPS

* Make sure you choose a fresh, ripe pineapple as it won't ripen any further when you get it home – once it has been cut from the tree it stops ripening.

* An easy way to tell if the fruit is fresh is to pull out a leaf – if it comes away easily the fruit is ready to eat.

METHOD

1. Using a large serrated knife, cut off the base and the leaves of the pineapple, so you have a flat top and bottom and the pineapple can balance on the cutting board.

2. Stand the fruit upright and, using a large serrated knife, cut the skin off in wide strips around the pineapple by cutting from top to bottom. Try to keep as much flesh on the fruit as you can.

3. With a small paring or fruit knife, work around the pineapple and pick out any spikes or skin left on the fruit.

4. To core the pineapple, cut it into quarters lengthwise and cut out the core from each slice with a large serrated knife.

54 PREPARING POMEGRANATE

The vibrant seeds of this exotic fruit can be pulped into a sauce or scattered over ice cream or salads for a burst of color and flavor.

TOOLS AND INGREDIENTS

Rolling pin   Fine strainer
Sharp chef's knife   Bowl
Cutting board   Pomegranates

METHOD

1. Gently hit the pomegranate with a rolling pin to loosen the seeds.

2. Cut the pomegranates in half, across the center of the fruit, not through the stalk.

3. Put a fine strainer over a bowl. Working over the bowl, push the skin of each pomegranate half inside out and use your fingers to pop the seeds out into the strainer.

EXPERT TIPS

* When choosing pomegranates, they should be a vibrant color and feel heavy, with bright, shiny skins.

* If you want to extract the juice to use in a sauce or in a dressing, use the back of a spoon to gently press the seeds down into the fine strainer – the juice will collect in the bowl.

4. Alternatively, you can turn the pomegranate halves upside down and tap the skin side with a wooden spoon. The seeds should fall out into the fine strainer.

55 SLICING MANGO

There are different ways to prepare a mango, depending on how you are going to use the fruit. This is the best technique for plenty of fruit without a lot of mess, as you will end up with large slices that can be cut further if need be.

METHOD

1. Firstly, peel the mango using a small sharp knife (see page 66).

2. Carefully slice the mango by cutting as close to the pit as possible on either side, so that you have two large slices.

3. Now you can slice the mango into the required size pieces. Try long strips, dice or shapes to vary the look of a fruit salad or accompaniment.

TOOLS AND INGREDIENTS

Sharp chef's knife
Cutting board
Mango

EXPERT TIPS

* Mango juice stains, so take care, or wear an apron.

* A ripe mango should give slightly and there should be a fruity aroma from the stem end. They continue to ripen when stored at room temperature so only refrigerate ripe fruit.

56 DICING MANGO

This is a technique that can be used to create a decorative fruit display, or to cut the mango into neat cubes for use in fruit salads or other recipes.

①

③

TOOLS AND INGREDIENTS

Sharp chef's knife
Cutting board

EXPERT TIPS

* It is important to use a sharp knife to score the flesh. Ripe mango can be very juicy so neat cuts are essential for the fruit cubes to hold their shape.

* If a mango is too ripe and soft to cube, purée the flesh and use it in smoothies, or as a sauce.

* Diced or sliced mango will keep for several days in the refrigerator or up to six months in the freezer.

METHOD

1. Slice the mango lengthwise either side of the pit, keeping the knife as close to the pit as possible. You should end up with two large pieces of mango.

2. Using a paring knife, cut a crisscross pattern into the flesh, cutting through to the skin but being careful not to pierce the skin.

3. Turn the mango inside out by pressing gently in the center of the skin side, so that the flesh pops out in an attractive cube pattern. You can either display the mango like this, or use a knife or teaspoon to scoop the cubes of mango from the skin.

4. Repeat with the second piece.

57 PEELING CITRUS FRUIT

Removing the peel from citrus fruit so that all the bitter pith is taken off and only the succulent flesh remains requires careful cutting techniques.

TOOLS AND INGREDIENTS

Sharp chef's knife
Cutting board
Citrus fruit

METHOD

1. Slice the top and bottom off the fruit, using a sharp chef's knife.

2. Stand the fruit upright on the cutting board, and slice downward in strips from top to bottom, removing peel and white pith and following the shape of the fruit. Work around the fruit so that all the peel is removed.

58 ZESTING CITRUS FRUIT

Fruit zest is used as a garnish for food and cocktails and to add a subtle citrus flavor to cooked dishes. The technique is to remove only the zest and none of the bitter white pith that lies just beneath it.

TOOLS AND INGREDIENTS

Zester
Fine grater
Citrus fruit

METHOD

1. Using a zester, peel off thin strips of zest by holding the fruit in one hand and pulling the zester toward you, working around the outside of the fruit.

2. For grated zest, gently rub the fruit along a fine grater.

> ### EXPERT TIPS
>
> * To make decorations for drinks or desserts, peel off the strips in long lengths. Wind the strips around a straw or a chopstick and hold for a minute or two.

59 SLICING CITRUS FRUIT

Slices of citrus fruit add a burst of color to desserts. Remember to add any juice on the cutting board to the dish for maximum flavor.

TOOLS AND INGREDIENTS

Serrated knife
Cutting board
Citrus fruit

METHOD

1. Peel the fruit (see page 66). Put the peeled fruit on its side so it stays in place on the cutting board.

2. Using a serrated knife, cut across the fruit into slices of desired thickness.

60 SEGMENTING CITRUS FRUIT

Fruit segments are a classic part of a fresh fruit salad or cocktail for breakfast or dessert.

TOOLS AND INGREDIENTS

Sharp chef's knife or
paring knife

Cutting board
Citrus fruit

METHOD

1. Peel the fruit (see page 66).

2. Hold the peeled fruit in the cupped palm of one hand. Use the white membrane as a guideline for where to make the cuts.

3. Using a sharp chef's knife or a paring knife, slice down one side of the white membrane, through to the core of the fruit; repeat on the other side. This will dislodge the fruit section between the membranes.

4. Rotate the fruit slightly in your hand and repeat, working your way around the fruit. Push the membranes under the thumb of the hand holding the fruit as you work.

61 PURÉEING BERRIES

This handy skill will help you transform ice cream, meringues and tarts. You can use one variety of berries, or combine a few varieties depending on what is in season.

TOOLS AND INGREDIENTS

Food mill (or blender)   Rubber spatula
Bowl   Berries (according to
Fine strainer   recipe)

METHOD

1. Set the food mill with the fine disk and place over a large bowl.

2. Put the berries in the mill and turn the handle continuously until all the fruit has passed through. You should be left with just the seeds in the mill and the lush fruit purée in the bowl.

3. Alternatively, put the berries in a blender or blend with a hand blender until the fruit has completely broken down.

4. Pour into a fine strainer over a bowl and rub with a rubber spatula until all the purée has been passed through.

EXPERT TIPS

* If stored in a sealed container, fruit purée will keep in the refrigerator for a couple of days. It makes a delicious topping for yogurt or oatmeal.

* Berries freeze well so stock up when they're in season. Freeze in a single layer on a baking sheet so that the fruit doesn't stick together. Once frozen, transfer to freezer bags or containers then simply defrost when you want to make fruit purée throughout the year.

62 BERRY COMPOTE

Fruit purée is blended raw fruit, whereas berry compote is cooked to concentrate the flavors, break down the fruit pulp and reduce the consistency.

TOOLS AND INGREDIENTS

Small pot
14 oz (400 g) berries
  (e.g., raspberries,
  blueberries,
  blackberries)

2 tbsp (30 ml) water
Cinnamon stick, star
  anise or vanilla bean

METHOD

1. Put 14 ounces (400 g) of berries in a small pot with 2 tablespoons (30 ml) of water and cook over a low heat.

2. Add either a cinnamon stick, a star anise or a vanilla bean (see expert tip) for flavor.

3. Simmer over a low heat until the berries are just collapsed, 5–10 minutes.

4. Serve either hot or cold.

EXPERT TIPS

* To prepare a vanilla bean, slide a small, sharp knife down the center of the bean cutting the vanilla bean in two, lengthwise. Now scrape the seeds from the bean and use in the recipe. If you want a subtle flavor, simply put the vanilla bean in whole — or use the skin of a vanilla bean that has had the seeds removed for a previous recipe.

* As with fruit purée, berry compote will keep in the refrigerator for a couple of days in a sealed container, and can be used to add a fruity zing to oatmeal or plain yogurt.

63 POACHING FRUIT IN SUGAR SYRUP

Fruit poached in a sugar syrup has a honeyed sweetness which makes it perfect for celebration desserts. Take care not to over-cook the fruit or burn yourself with the boiling sugar.

METHOD

1. Add your chosen fruit to a pot of simmering sugar syrup (see page 32). Ensure the fruit is completely covered so that it cooks evenly and each piece soaks up some of the liquid.

2. Poach the fruit for approximately 10–20 minutes. The exact time will depend on the variety of fruit and its ripeness but it should be very tender while still retaining its shape.

3. Carefully remove the fruit with a slotted spoon. You now can increase the temperature and reduce the syrup to a thick, sticky consistency to serve over the fruit.

TOOLS AND INGREDIENTS

Large pot
Slotted spoon
Sugar syrup (see
  page 32)
Fruit (according to recipe)

EXPERT TIPS

* The syrup will sweeten and tenderize the fruit and it can be served on its own as a dessert, with a little of the reduced syrup spooned over. Alternatively, it can be used to make fruit pies or tarts.

* Use this method for larger fruit such as peaches or pears, or for small fruit, such as plums. Adjust cooking time and watch to ensure fruit does not break down.

64 POACHING FRUIT IN WINE

This technique works especially well with pears and other large, solid fruit that can handle intense heat but remain intact. You can use red or white wine for this technique – red wine will impart a wonderfully rich color to the fruit, something to keep in mind when choosing.

METHOD

1. Peel and core the pears (see pages 66–67). If you want to keep the stems intact, poach the pears whole.

2. Heat the wine and water over a medium heat. Add a cinnamon stick, vanilla bean or star anise to the pot. Add the sugar and stir until dissolved.

3. Add the prepared pears to the pot and bring the liquid to a gentle simmer.

4. Poach the pears for 10–20 minutes, depending on the ripeness of the fruit.

5. Remove with a slotted spoon. You can now reduce the wine until it is a thick syrup and serve this over the fruit as a sauce.

TOOLS AND INGREDIENTS

Large pot
Slotted spoon
4 pears (or other large fruit)
1 bottle red or white wine

Cinnamon stick, vanilla bean or star anise
7 fl oz (200 ml) water
½ cup (110 g) white sugar

EXPERT TIPS

* Serve these poached pears as a simple dessert with a spoon of mascarpone or ice cream.

65 BAKING FRUIT

This is a delicious way to concentrate the flavor of fruit and it works particularly well with apples or peaches.

TOOLS AND INGREDIENTS

Sharp chef's knife
Baking dish
Fruit (e.g., apples or
  peaches)

METHOD (WHOLE FRUIT)

1. Core your chosen fruit (see page 67).

2. Score around the middle of the fruit to stop the flesh from bursting out of the skin during baking.

3. Stuff the core with your choice of filling (see expert tips).

4. Put the stuffed fruit, standing upright and close together, in a baking dish and bake for about 20 minutes, until the fruit is tender but still holds its shape.

EXPERT TIPS

* Filling the cavity of the fruit will add extra flavor that will seep into the flesh during the cooking process. Try a combination of raisins and cranberries mixed with a little rum or brandy, and sprinkled with brown sugar and cinnamon, with baked apples or pears.

METHOD (HALVED FRUIT)

1. Halve the fruit and scoop out the core or pit (see pages 68–69).

2. Fill the hollowed out space with your choice of filling (see expert tips).

3. Put the filled fruit in a compact baking dish and bake for about 15 minutes, until the fruit is tender but still holds its shape.

66 BLANCHING AND SKINNING NUTS

When nuts are shelled there is still a thin layer of skin between the shell and the nut, which is not unpleasant but the nut will look better without it. However, when cooking with nuts, it is important to blanch them first; otherwise the unsightly skins will detach during the cooking process and will be left as a residue in the dish.

TOOLS AND INGREDIENTS

Heatproof bowl
Selection of nuts (e.g.,
  almonds, pistachios)

METHOD

1. Put the nuts in a large heatproof bowl.

2. Cover with boiling water and leave to stand for 1-2 minutes.

3. Drain the nuts, fill the bowl with cold water, or rinse the nuts under the cold tap. This stops the "cooking" process and makes them easier to peel.

4. Once the nuts are cool enough to handle, peel the skin off with your fingers; it should slide off easily.

EXPERT TIPS

* The key to this technique is to immerse the nuts in cold water immediately after blanching.

* Don't leave the nuts in the boiling water for too long or they will start to absorb moisture and lose their crunch.

67 TOASTING AND SKINNING NUTS

This technique works in a similar way to blanching nuts (see page 81) but whereas blanching retains the natural flavor of the nut, toasting gives the nuts a smoky flavor and a crispier texture.

TOOLS AND INGREDIENTS

Baking sheet
Clean dish towel
Selection of nuts

EXPERT TIPS

* Once the nuts are toasted, you can eat them whole or crush them to use in other recipes such as sprinkled over ice cream or tarts, or added to cookie or cake mixes.

METHOD

1. Preheat the oven to 350°F (175°C).

2. Put your selection of shelled nuts on a baking sheet. They should be in a single layer so that they are all toasted uniformly. If you have a lot of nuts, you can use two baking sheets.

3. Toast in the oven for approximately 10 minutes, moving the nuts around several times to ensure they toast all over. To do this you can just give the baking sheet a little shake.

4. Remove the baking sheets from the oven and tip the nuts into a clean dish towel. Wrap them up and leave for a few minutes.

5. Rub the nuts in the dish towel and the skins should fall off.

68 DRY- OR PAN-TOASTING NUTS

This is another method of dry toasting nuts. It's a bit quicker than waiting for the oven to preheat so it's ideal for a quick snack.

METHOD

1. Heat a heavy skillet on the stove.

2. Once hot, add the selection of nuts in a single layer, ensuring there is space to move the nuts around to toast all over. You may need to do this in two or more batches.

3. Toast the nuts over the heat for about 5 minutes. Move the nuts around frequently by gently shaking the skillet, until they are a golden toasted color. Don't worry if they are not uniformly brown, this method results in some mottling but this doesn't affect the flavor of the nuts.

TOOLS AND INGREDIENTS

Heavy skillet
Selection of nuts

MEAT SKILLS

There are certain key knife and preparation skills that are essential to learn when cooking meat. For example, knowing where the cuts come from on the animal, and which cuts work best for certain recipes, is key to creating successful meat dishes. Certain cuts need long, slow cooking to draw out the flavor and tenderize the meat, while others need no more than a quick moment on the skillet to enjoy the flavor that succulent meat offers.

As with all food, the rule "quality over quantity" applies. Far better to buy good quality meat from a reputable retailer less often than to buy cheap in order to put meat on the table every night.

In this chapter you will learn about different cuts of meat – their names and locations – as well as the best ways to trim meat, butterfly, check for doneness, and how to correctly carve a joint.

69 CUTS OF BEEF

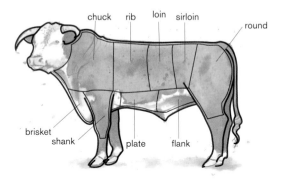

It is important to buy meat that is fresh, ideally organic, local and well-reared. It's great to build up a relationship with a butcher or producer at farmers' markets. They will appreciate the community support but these are also the people who will know most about the origin of the beef you are buying. They will always have the best advice about cuts and cooking techniques and will be able to prepare the meat for you exactly the way you want it.

When choosing beef, the smell should not be strong – it should smell fresh. High quality meat should have an even marbling of fat and should be a deep red color. The outer layer of fat should be smooth and have a creamy white color.

It is best to buy meat right when you need it, rather than bulk buying and freezing it for later. This is not only more economical but it also means that you are cooking with the freshest meat possible. When preparing beef, any bones should be cleanly cut, and the excess fat and sinew should be trimmed, leaving a neat cut of beef.

Chuck Eye Steak

- Marbled with some fat – this is a lean cut
- Can be sold boned or cubed
- Ideal for long, slow cooking

Porterhouse Steak

- Thicker cut than the T-bone steak and has much more of the tenderloin relative to the loin portion
- Perfect broiled but can be sautéed or pan-fried

Brisket Cut

- Rolled and boned
- Ideal for long and slow cooking – salted and poached

Flank Cut

- Barbecue or broil as a whole piece
- More economical cut but extremely flavorsome and lean, with even marbling

Rib Cut

- Lean cut with layers of fat
- Cooked on the bone to help tenderize the meat and to retain flavor and juices
- Ideal for roasting, sliced into individual steaks on the bone, braised or pot-roasted (when boned and rolled)

Shank (Shin) Cut

- Delicious meaty flavor
- Cook with bone marrow for additional flavor
- Flavor is maximized by long and slow cooking

Rib-Entrecote Steak

- This is a boned steak from a rib cut
- Premium cut of beef so often expensive
- Perfect gently pan-fried

Rib-Fore Roast

- Lean meat with a layer of fat around the outside
- Ideal for slow cooking/ braising or roasting

Skirt

- Prized for its flavor rather than tenderness
- Marinate before grilling or pan-sear very quickly

T-Bone Steak

- Suited to fast, dry heat cooking methods, such as broiling
- Considered one of the highest quality steaks, so expensive

Tenderloin Steak (Fillet)

- Tenderest part of the beef
- Cut for steaks or roasts

Top Sirloin Steak

- Steaks: T-bone, sirloin, porterhouse (thicker cut)
- Very tender meat – lean with low fat content
- Can be cooked on or off the bone

70 CUTTING BEEF

Different cuts of beef call for different knife skills but some techniques apply to all cuts. Meat should be treated carefully and the way you cut it can have a big impact on the appearance of the meat, as well as how it cooks in different recipes.

METHOD (SLICING)

1. Put the piece of beef on a cutting board.

2. Using a sharp chef's knife, slice the piece of beef across the grain (see expert tips) into slices of required thickness. For example, you might require steaks or you might want the beef to be cut into thin slices.

EXPERT TIPS

* Cutting against the grain simply means that you are cutting the meat in the opposite direction of the sinewy fibers that naturally occur in most cuts of meat. These fibers can be tough and difficult to chew, particularly in recipes where the meat is only cooked for a short period of time (lengthy cooking times will break down the fibers and make them softer and easier to chew). When making cuts into the meat, look for the direction the fibers are running and cut across them, rather than following the lines.

TOOLS AND INGREDIENTS

Sharp chef's knife
Cutting board

Beef (cut depending on recipe)

METHOD (STRIPS)

1 Begin with the piece of beef lying flat on a cutting board. Using a sharp chef's knife, slice the meat into thin, even slices.

2 Lay each slice on the board and cut them vertically, into thin, even strips. This technique is ideal for use in dishes such as stir-fries.

METHOD (DICING)

1 As with the previous techniques, place the piece of beef on a cutting board. Using a sharp chef's knife, slice the meat into equal slices of required thickness.

2 Cut one slice at a time into equal-size strips and then cut the strips into cubes or dice (depending on the recipe).

71 COOKING STEAK

Many people order steak in a restaurant but wouldn't dream of cooking it at home as the results are never as good. However, with a few simple guidelines, you can cook restaurant-quality steaks from the comfort of your own kitchen.

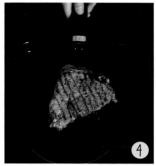

TOOLS AND INGREDIENTS

Sharp chef's knife
Cutting board
Griddle

Steak (according to recipe)
Salt and black pepper

METHOD

1. Season a room-temperature steak with salt and pepper on both sides.

2. Heat a griddle over a medium-high heat until smoking hot.

3. Put the steak on the griddle and flip over once there are griddle marks on the underside of the meat (see opposite for checking for doneness). Cook on the other side until it also has griddle marks.

4. Turn the steak over again at a 45° angle to the grill pan to create a diamond effect on the underside of the steak.

5. Repeat on the other side.

EXPERT TIPS

* Steak tends to cook better if you begin with it at room temperature: the meat relaxes and will cook evenly.

* A damp piece of meat will cook but you won't achieve the slightly crispy crust on the outside so always pat the meat dry with paper towels before cooking.

72 CHECKING FOR DONENESS

When it comes to cooking times for steak, it is really a case of personal opinion – while one person will only accept a steak that has been flashed briefly in a skillet, someone else will choose a well-done piece of meat. However, there are certain techniques for getting cooking times just right – whatever your preference.

TOOLS AND INGREDIENTS

Sharp chef's knife
Cutting board
Grill pan
Steak (according to
    recipe)
Salt and pepper

EXPERT TIPS

* Once you have cooked the steak, set it aside to rest for a couple of minutes before serving. This allows the meat to reabsorb the juices so that the meat is succulent to eat.

* It sounds obvious but a good steak starts with good meat so always buy good-quality steak.

METHOD

1. To check to see how cooked a steak is, touch is the best measuring device: the firmer the steak, the more cooked it is.

2. As a guideline, you cook a steak (see opposite) for approximately 2–3 minutes each side for rare, 3–4 minutes each side for medium-rare and 5–6 minutes each side for well done.

3. A quick way to gauge the firmness of a steak in comparison to its doneness, is to press your index, middle and ring finger along the pad and base of your thumb. The pressure under your index finger is the same as a rare steak, whereas the firmer pressure under the ring finger equates to well done. The pressure under your middle finger is the same as medium-rare.

73 CARVING A ROLLED JOINT

A rolled joint makes an ideal choice for family roast. If you buy your meat from the butcher, they will advise you of the best cut and will debone and roll the joint for you so it is simple to cook.

TOOLS AND INGREDIENTS

Carving knife
Carving fork
Kitchen shears
Cutting board

Roast rolled joint of meat

EXPERT TIPS

* The meat will cool slightly while it is resting but if you serve piping hot gravy this will reheat the meat when you serve it.

METHOD

1. When the meat has cooked, remove it from the oven and set aside to rest. This allows the meat to reabsorb the juices, making it moist and succulent when served.

2. Once the meat has rested, remove the twine that has trussed the joint. Cut through the twine in a number of places so the meat is not damaged, and carefully remove the twine. Check that all of the twine has been removed.

3. Using a carving knife, slice across the joint in thick, even slices. Use the carving knife to keep the meat steady while you cut.

4. You can either place slices on individual serving plates or arrange the meat on a large serving platter.

74 CARVING A JOINT

There is something wonderfully comforting about sitting around the dining table as a joint of meat is carved. It conjures up childhood memories and is all about sharing good food with family and friends.

TOOLS AND INGREDIENTS

Cutting board
Carving knife
Carving fork
Cooked joint of meat
(e.g., rib of beef)

EXPERT TIPS

* After each slice, use the flat side of the knife to transfer the meat to the serving plate – this will ensure the slices don't break.

* A spiked cutting board or platter will help to keep the meat steady while you carve. Some boards also feature a recessed edge, which holds the juices – these can then be used to make gravy.

METHOD

1. When the meat has cooked, remove it from the oven and set aside to rest. This allows the meat to reabsorb the juices, making it moist and succulent when served.

2. Put the joint of meat upright on a large board, with the bones facing upward.

3. Place a carving fork in the base of the meat to keep it steady and hold it there with one hand. Using the carving knife, carve the meat off the bone that separates it from the rib, keeping as close to the bone as possible.

4. Now put the joint flat side down on the board and carve across the joint in slices of the desired thickness.

5. Arrange the slices on individual serving plates or a large serving platter.

75 CUTS OF LAMB

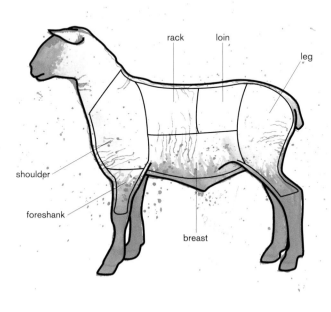

rack   loin   leg

shoulder

foreshank

breast

Good quality lamb should have a dark pink color, be firm to the touch and have a fine grain to its texture. There should be marbling across the meat and the fat on the outside should be creamy white and firm to the touch. The skin on larger joints should feel moist and firm. Lamb is aged between three and twelve months, and mutton is meat from animals older than 1 year: it has a stronger taste and the flesh is a darker color.

Chump Chop

- Cut taken from the lower back
- Sold as chops or, with the bone removed, as steaks
- Ideal for broiling and barbecues or slow cooked in the oven

Loin Chop (Boneless)

- Boneless loin chops (or noisettes) create a smart dish when pan-fried and served pink
- Tender, lean and with succulent flavor

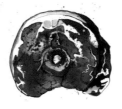

Neck of Lamb (Bone-in)

- Even marbling of fat across the meat
- Outer layer of fat
- Best cooked on the bone
- Requires long and slow cooking or braising

Breast

- One of the least expensive cuts
- Full of flavor and needs to be cooked slowly
- Quite a fatty cut, but during cooking the fat melts off and can be poured away

Primal Leg

- Classic and popular joint – more expensive
- Lean meat with even marbling of fat
- Even layer of outer fat
- Can be butterflied, making it flatter – ideal for barbecuing, or rolled and stuffed

Loin

- Can be roasted whole or separated into single or double loin chops, sirloin chops, or cut into noisettes
- Sirloin and loin chops are ideal for broiling and barbecuing – lean meat with low ratio of marbling
- Cooking on the bone improves the flavor and moisture
- Sirloin roast is lean meat with outer layer of fat that should be trimmed before cooking – ideal for slow cooking and roasting

Rack

- Prime cut so expensive
- Whole rack consists of eight ribs, neatly trimmed of fat
- Perfect roasted until pink

Shank

- Meaty cut from the lower end of the leg
- Tender cut that falls from the bone after slow cooking

Shoulder

- Deep rich flavor and color; can be fatty
- Good cut for slow cooking – benefits from slow roasting
- Also good when cubed and braised or boned and rolled – good for stuffing

Rib Chops

- Individual ribs cut from the rack

76 BONING A SHOULDER OF LAMB

This rich, succulent cut is ideal for slow roasting or braising. The long cooking time helps to break down the fat and sinew, which adds to the flavor of the dish but which can be tough to eat after shorter cooking times. Shoulder is often used in stews, casseroles and curries as it can stand up to punchy flavors.

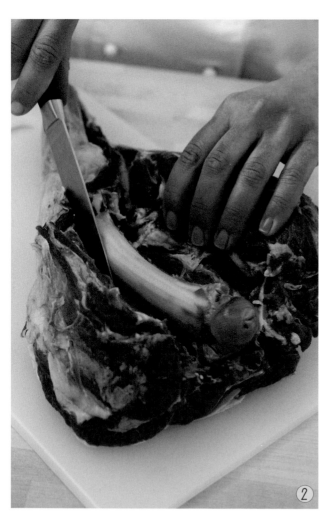

TOOLS AND INGREDIENTS

Sharp boning knife
Large cutting board
Shoulder of lamb

METHOD

1. Put the shoulder of lamb, skin side down, on a large board.

2. Use a sharp boning knife to cut along either side of the large, flat blade bone.

3. Next cut around and under the ball and socket joint at the end of the blade bone to separate it from the shoulder bone.

4. Make sure the shoulder is placed so that the blade bone is running toward you. Place one hand firmly on the meat to hold it in place and pull the blade bone firmly away from the meat – it should come away cleanly.

5. Cut around the shoulder bone, making sure to scrape away all the meat with the blade of the knife. It should be pulled off easily.

6. If there are any pieces of meat left around the bone, pull or slice these away.

EXPERT TIPS

∗ Use the bone and any small pieces of meat to make a lamb broth. The best way to make lamb broth is to roast the bones in a hot oven (390°F/200°C) for about 1 hour. Meanwhile, in a large pan, fry 1 chopped onion, 1 garlic clove, 1 chopped carrot and 1 chopped celery stick in a little oil. Add the cooked bones to the pot, add a dash of white wine and cover with water. Simmer the broth gently for 3 hours then strain through a fine strainer. You will have enough to be able to use some immediately and freeze the rest in portions.

77 BUTTERFLYING A LEG OF LAMB

A butterfly cut is basically a boned leg of lamb. You can ask the butcher to do this for you and a number of stores now stock butterflied legs of lamb. However, butterflying is a basic knife skill that is a handy addition to your culinary knowledge.

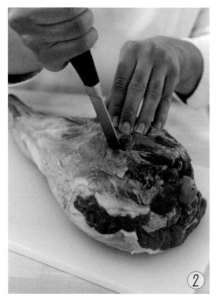
②

③

③

TOOLS AND INGREDIENTS

Boning knife
Large cutting board
Leg of lamb

METHOD

1 Put the leg of lamb on a large board so that it lies vertically along the length of the board.

2 Using a boning knife, cut down the length of the leg, along one side of the bone, keeping as close to the bone as possible but being careful not to slice all the way through the meat. Repeat on the other side.

3. Cut under the bone.

4. Cut all around the bone to remove it.

5. The meat should now be open flat. Make deep slashes into the meat at regular intervals, but don't cut all the way through.

6. Make sure the meat is roughly of even thickness all the way across so that it cooks evenly. If there are thicker sections you can trim these.

EXPERT TIPS

* The blade of a boning knife is flexible and will enable you to remove as much meat as possible from the bone.

* This cut is ideal for marinating. Once the marinade has been rubbed in, transfer the meat to the refrigerator for a couple of hours to allow the flavors to soak into the meat.

* Cook the marinated meat in a hot oven or over searing coals on a barbecue. The skin should form a crispy crust, while the meat inside is tender and juicy. Baste with the marinade while cooking and serve the lamb in thick slices with a yogurt or chili sauce.

78 CARVING A LEG OF LAMB

It is important to carve a leg of lamb correctly in order to achieve even slices and to get as much meat off the bone as possible. The leg is more difficult to cut than the loin, as there are fibers running in different directions so it will take a little practice to perfect your carving skills.

TOOLS AND INGREDIENTS

Carving knife
Carving fork

Large cutting board
Cooked leg of lamb

METHOD

1. After allowing the cooked leg of lamb to rest, put it on a large cutting board. Use a carving knife to cut vertically into the knuckle end (nearer to the exposed bone end) of the leg. Use the carving fork to hold the joint steady as you cut.

2. Now cut horizontally into the first cut so that you remove a wedge of meat.

3. Carve along both sides of the bone to remove slices of meat and transfer to a serving platter to keep the board clear.

4. Turn the leg over and slice off the remaining meat, cutting on a slight angle.

EXPERT TIPS

* An alternative method is to carve away larger pieces of meat, working around the bone. Next slice each piece into slices of required size.

* Use the bone and any small pieces of meat to make lamb broth (see expert tip, page 97).

79 PREPARING A RACK OF LAMB

A rack of lamb makes an impressive dinner party showpiece. Although there is a little preparation work involved, it is fairly straightforward and the results speak for themselves. Keep accompaniments simple and fresh – mashed potato or celeriac and steamed greens – and allow the lamb to be the star of the dinner plate.

EXPERT TIPS

* When you buy the lamb, make sure there is an even number of ribs – it will make it easier when it comes to dividing the chops for serving.

TOOLS AND INGREDIENTS

Boning knife
Large cutting board
Rack of lamb

METHOD

1. Put the lamb upright on a large board. Use a boning knife to cut downward to remove the backbone (chine) in one piece.

2. Now put the lamb, skin side facing upward, on the board and trim the fat from the small bones – it should come off in one whole piece.

3. Turn the meat over onto the skin side and score the meat between the small bones.

4. Cut and trim away the meat and fat from between the bones. This is called "French trimming" and is important for presentation.

5. You can either leave the rack of lamb whole for cooking, or cut neatly and evenly between the bones to separate into individual chops.

80 CUTS OF PORK

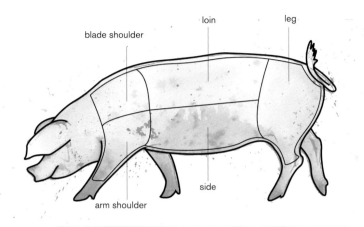

Pork is a versatile meat that lends itself to many cooking styles, including curing and smoking. When choosing pork, look for meat that is pink in color and has a firm, white layer of fat. The meat itself should feel moist without being slimy or damp. Your butcher will give you advice on the best cuts for the recipes you want to make but make sure that larger joints are prepared well, are neatly trimmed, and look freshly cut.

Breeds have become very important, with many people becoming aware of traditional breeds such as Lacombe, Tamworth etc. The origin and flavor of meat is tied up in breeds and farmers and butchers are concerned about promoting sustainable meat, and also breeding rarer breeds, as they become more popular.

Bacon

- Can be smoked or unsmoked, streaky or back
- Can be dry cured by rubbing the meat in salt and flavorings (such as spices or honey), or wet-cured by soaking the meat in brine

Flat Bone Ribs

- Also known as button ribs
- Consist of the last four to six bones on the backbone
- Perfect for barbecuing

Fore Loin Chop

- The fore loin produces pork cutlets, perfect for broiling or barbecuing

Hock

- Consists of much skin, tendons and ligaments, so requires long cooking through stewing or braising to be made palatable and to release its distinctive flavor

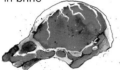

Loin Chop (Bone-in)

- Marbled meat on the bone, with a thin layer of fat – tender and juicy
- Ideal for barbecuing, pan-frying or broiling

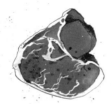

Loin Chop (Boneless)

- Less fatty than the bone-in loin chop but less flavorsome
- Ideal for barbecuing, pan-frying or broiling

Belly Pork

- Popular cut with thick layer of fat and equal proportion of meat
- When cooked well, the fat is completely edible and delicious as it has a very soft, melting quality

Leg

- Good for roasting whole, or dicing and cooking slowly

Arm Shoulder

- Slightly neglected cut but better value than pork belly
- Ideal for long marinating and slow cooking or brining (pulled pork)

Spare Ribs

- Ideal for barbecuing – good value
- Ideal for long marinating
- Perfect broiled or roasted

Tenderloin

- Prime cut that is very lean with almost no fat
- Moist and tender meat
- Benefits from shorter cooking

Loin

- Very lean meat with thin layer of outer fat
- Good for roasting and braising
- Popular cut is rolled center loin roast

81 ROASTING PORK WITH STUFFING

Roast pork with crackling has to be one of life's great pleasures. Stuffing the pork adds extra flavor and it also helps to keep the meat moist. Prepare the stuffing in advance and chill in the refrigerator until required.

TOOLS AND INGREDIENTS

Sharp chef's knife
Large cutting board
Kitchen twine
Pork loin roast

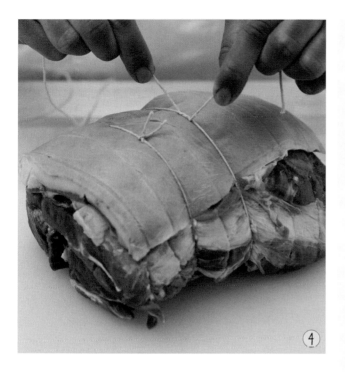

(4)

METHOD

1. Put the pork loin on a large board, skin side down.

2. Cut down the center of the loin, about three-quarters of the way through the meat, being careful not to cut through the meat entirely.

3. Fill the cavity with your stuffing of choice (see expert tips) packing the stuffing in tightly but leaving a little gap at either end of the loin so the stuffing doesn't leak out during cooking.

EXPERT TIPS

* When you leave the meat to rest after cooking, leave the twine in place to maintain the shape of the loin. Remove the twine and cut into thick slices before serving.

* To make sure your pork loin has perfect crackling, pat the skin dry with paper towels and score the skin before you begin preparing the meat. Cut regularly spaced, even scores into the skin, being careful not to cut through to the meat. Sprinkle with salt.

* It's easy to make your own stuffing and certain ingredients naturally go well together. Sage and onion is the obvious example, but for something a little different, try one of the following:

  Chopped apple and apricot
  Apple and date
  Bacon and sausage meat
  Fresh herbs and baked apple

4. Roll the pork loin lengthwise from one side into a tight roll, then truss with kitchen twine.

5. Put the pork in a roasting pan and cook according to the recipe instructions.

POULTRY SKILLS

Chicken is a popular ingredient: it offers good value for money, it is healthy and it is also extremely versatile. From roast chicken for a family lunch to chicken breasts served in sauce, and from thigh meat cooked for lengthy periods in rich curry sauces to legs marinated and grilled on the barbecue, it's no wonder that poultry features so often on our shopping lists.

Over the course of this chapter, you will discover some of the basic skills that will help you increase your poultry preparation skills and diversify your recipe repertoire. For example, a spatchcock chicken or poussin elevates the humble bird to dinner party status, while escallops are a favorite with kids. From trussing to stuffing, you will find all the techniques and skills you need on the following pages.

82 REMOVING THE WISHBONE

A chicken without a wishbone is easier to carve. It was traditionally removed after eating the bird, when two people would pull it apart – the person with the bigger piece being allowed to make a wish. However it is best to remove it while the chicken is still raw, as you will reap the benefits of improved carving skills that way.

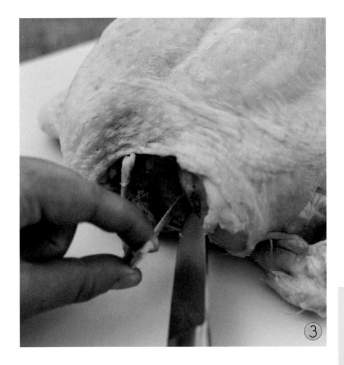

TOOLS AND INGREDIENTS

Cutting board
Boning knife
Whole chicken

METHOD

1. Put the chicken on a board, with the legs facing away from you.

2. Push back any excess skin from the neck of the chicken.

3. Cut around the wishbone with a boning knife.

4. Scrape any meat away from the wishbone, and then cut it away from the chicken, removing it from the base.

EXPERT TIPS

* Pull out both parts of the bone at the same time, otherwise it could snap and you will have to feel around for the remaining piece.

* If you still want to make a wish place the wishbone in the pan to cook with the bird and present it at the table.

83 TRUSSING A CHICKEN

A trussed chicken will hold its shape while cooking, which makes this technique ideal for cooking stuffed birds. It is used when presentation is important and you want to serve the whole, cooked bird at the dinner table (remember to remove the twine before serving.)

 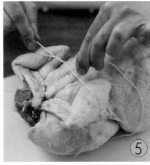

TOOLS AND INGREDIENTS

Cutting board
Kitchen twine
Whole chicken

EXPERT TIPS

* Always cut a longer length of kitchen twine than you think you will need: it is easier to trim away the excess at the end than to have to start again if you run out of twine.

* This technique can be used for other poultry or game birds.

METHOD

1. Put the chicken on a board, breast side up with the legs facing away from you.

2. Tie kitchen twine around the legs, being sure to tuck any excess skin at the tail end under the legs.

3. Pull the twine toward you (the neck end of the chicken), ensuring that it lies between the breasts and legs.

4. Turn the chicken over and cross the twine so that it comes under and around the wings of the chicken.

5. Tie the twine tightly, making sure that the wings are pulled in securely. Trim the twine and prepare the chicken for the oven.

84 STUFFING A CHICKEN

Whether you are simply putting a lemon wedge inside the chicken cavity, or you are preparing a homemade stuffing to cook and serve alongside the chicken, stuffing adds depth of flavor to the meat.

METHOD

1. If you stuff the whole cavity tightly, it will take longer for the bird to cook and the stuffing itself might not cook through properly. Therefore it is best to just stuff the neck end with stuffing – either sausage meat or other homemade stuffing. This is optional.

2. Put several sprigs of parsley into the cavity of the chicken.

3. Next put half a lemon into the cavity.

4. If you want to keep the flavor and ingredients safely inside the chicken, you can truss it (see page 109). This will also help to hold the shape of the chicken during cooking.

TOOLS AND INGREDIENTS

Sharp chef's knife
Cutting board
Whole chicken

Stuffing of choice
Parsley sprigs
Lemon

EXPERT TIPS

* Less is more when it comes to stuffing: even if you are stuffing the whole chicken cavity, use small balls of stuffing or just a little mixture, rather than packing it in too tightly.

85 SPATCHCOCKING A CHICKEN

Spatchcocking looks impressive and it works equally well for most poultry and game birds. The technique involves removing the back and breast bones so that the chicken can be laid out flat. This works particularly well if you are going to griddle or barbecue the chicken as marinade can be brushed over the chicken and the meat will cook more quickly and evenly than it would if roasting.

EXPERT TIPS

* Remember to adjust your cooking times if you are using this technique for a roast chicken recipe – a spatchcock chicken will cook much more quickly.

TOOLS AND INGREDIENTS

Cutting board
Poultry shears or large
  kitchen shears

Sharp chef's knife
Whole chicken

METHOD

1. Put the chicken on a board, breast side down.

2. Using poultry shears or large kitchen shears, cut along each side of the backbone, and remove it from the chicken.

3. Open out the chicken and use your hand to locate the breastbone. Using a sharp chef's knife, cut along either side of the bone, taking care not to cut right through the flesh. Pull the bone out and spread the chicken out flat.

4. Alternatively, turn the chicken over and push down firmly with the heel of your hand to break the breastbone and the chicken will then be easy to flatten. The chicken can now be prepared for cooking.

86 REMOVING THE SKIN FROM A CHICKEN BREAST

Crispy chicken skin might taste delicious but it is also the fattiest part of the chicken so if you are aiming for a healthier recipe it is best to remove it before cooking. Skin-on chicken breasts are often less expensive in the supermarket so this is a quick way to economize. It takes a little practice but is easy once you get the hang of it.

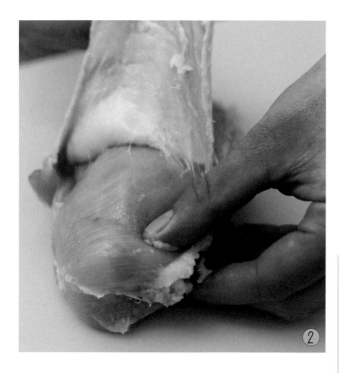

METHOD

1 Put the chicken breast skin side up on a cutting board.

2 Lift the skin at the point furthest from you. Hold the chicken breast firmly with one hand and use the other hand to pull the skin upward and backward toward you. It should lift off easily.

TOOLS AND INGREDIENTS

Cutting board
Chicken breast

EXPERT TIPS

* Chicken skin can be greasy; if this is the case, use a paper towel to help get a firm grip on the skin.

* If the skin is difficult to lift from the end of the chicken breast, you can use a knife to begin separating it, then use your fingers when there is enough skin for a firm grip.

87 BONING A CHICKEN LEG

The darker leg meat on a chicken is preferable for certain recipes, especially those that require longer cooking times. For some recipes, it is best to remove the bone first and this simple technique will make it easy.

TOOLS AND INGREDIENTS

Sharp chef's knife
Cutting board
Chicken leg

METHOD

1. Take a whole chicken leg and put it on a board, skin side down.

2. Using a chef's knife, cut down along the bone running from the drumstick, keeping as close to the bone as possible. Continue down to the drumstick, working slowly and methodically to produce a clean cut.

3. Repeat this process along the other side of the bone.

4. Pull the bone up, scraping away any excess skin that attaches the bone to the meat as you work.

5. Cut away the bone from the drumstick end. It should be clean of meat and come out easily. You may need to cut around the base of the bone in order to remove it.

EXPERT TIPS

* Once you have de-boned the chicken leg, you can stuff it (a ballottine) or you can score it with a sharp knife and cook on a griddle or on the barbecue.

113

88 CUTTING ESCALLOPS

Crispy crumb-coated chicken escallops are easy to prepare and a great family favorite.

TOOLS AND INGREDIENTS

Cutting board
Sharp chef's knife
Parchment paper

Rolling pin
Chicken breasts

EXPERT TIPS

* To cook a chicken escallop, liberally sprinkle seasoned flour onto a large plate and whisk two eggs in a flat bowl. Put some bread crumbs on another plate. Season the chicken slices, then dip each one in the flour, then the egg and finally the bread crumbs so they are coated all over. Heat a little oil in a skillet and cook the chicken for about 2–3 minutes on each side, until they are cooked through and the bread crumbs are golden.

METHOD

1. Put a skinless chicken breast on a cutting board.

2. Using a sharp chef's knife, slice thinly across the breast on an angle to produce two, thin slices.

3. Put the chicken slices, one at a time, between sheets of folded parchment paper. Hit the chicken firmly with a rolling pin until it is evenly flattened. Transfer to a plate and repeat with the remaining slices.

4. These can be breaded and fried (see expert tips, left).

89 CUTTING INTO STRIPS

Chicken strips are ideal for stir-fries or pasta dishes, as they cook quickly and can be used with a number of different ingredients and flavors.

TOOLS AND INGREDIENTS

Sharp chef's knife
Cutting board

Chicken escallops (see opposite)

METHOD

1 Form the chicken into escallops (see opposite).

2 Using a sharp chef's knife, thinly slice each escallop into strips.

90 REMOVING TENDONS

The tendons on chicken are tough and sinewy and not pleasant to eat so it is worth spending the time removing them before cooking.

TOOLS AND INGREDIENTS

Small paring knife
Cutting board

Chicken breast

METHOD

1 Using a small paring knife, cut under the white tendon that runs along the underside of the chicken breast.

2 Now cut over the tendon and use your fingers to pull it up and away from the rest of the chicken breast.

EXPERT TIPS

* If you can locate the end of the tendon another method of removal is to pull it out with your fingers. You can use a knife to loosen any particularly stubborn sections.

91 CUTTING CHICKEN BREASTS IN HALF

Cutting chicken breasts in half is a useful skill if you are preparing food for children or if you fancy a smaller portion.

TOOLS AND INGREDIENTS

Large sharp chef's knife
Cutting board
Chicken breasts

METHOD

1 There are two ways to cut a chicken breast in half: you can cut lengthwise through the breast in order to create large, thin slices or prepare escallops; or you can cut crosswise through the center of the chicken breast to create two large, chunky pieces of chicken.

2 If slicing crosswise, use a large, sharp chef's knife and cut through the chicken breast, following the grain if possible, to keep the halves neat. Ensure that both pieces are the same size so that they cook evenly.

92 DICING CHICKEN THIGHS

Diced chicken thighs are tasty in stir-fries or pasta dishes.

TOOLS AND INGREDIENTS

Sharp chef's knife
Cutting board
Chicken thighs

METHOD

1 Firstly, remove the chicken skin by pulling it off the thigh (see page 112).

2 If the thigh still has the bone in, remove this. Use a sharp chef's knife to slice down either side of the bone, being careful not to slice all the way through to the other side of the thigh. Use your fingers to pull the bone out, slicing underneath with the knife, if necessary.

3 Lay the thigh out flat and cut it into even slices. Now dice the meat into pieces of the required size.

93 JOINTING A CHICKEN INTO 4 PIECES

An essential skill when cooking with chicken. Buying a whole chicken is often much cheaper than buying the wings, legs, breasts etc. separately, so mastering this skill will save you money.

 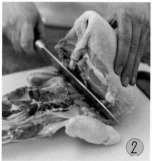 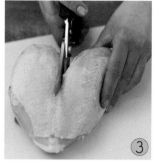 

TOOLS AND INGREDIENTS

Cutting board
Large chef's knife
Whole chicken

Poultry shears

METHOD

1. Place chicken on the board, breast facing up and the neck end facing toward you.

2. Using a large chef's knife, cut horizontally between the rib cages of the chicken, starting from the neck. Cut through completely so that you have the breast bone as a separate piece.

3. Cut along the breastbone with poultry shears to halve the carcass. You will need to use some pressure to do this.

94 CHICKEN SUPREME

This is a boneless breast with the wing and skin.

METHOD

1. Joint a chicken (see above.) At the final step, separate the legs but leave the wing tip attached.

EXPERT TIPS

* Make sure the knife is very sharp as the carcass is difficult to cut through.

95 JOINTING A CHICKEN INTO 6 PIECES

Jointing a chicken in this way is ideal for casseroles and stews.

TOOLS AND INGREDIENTS

Sharp chef's knife
Cutting board
Whole chicken

METHOD

1. Work through all the steps for jointing a chicken into 4 pieces (see page 117).

2. To separate the thigh and drumstick, put the leg on the board, skin side down, and cut through the line of white fat that separates the two.

96 JOINTING A CHICKEN INTO 8 PIECES

If you want smaller pieces of chicken in your dish, joint into 8 pieces as follows.

TOOLS AND INGREDIENTS

Sharp chef's knife
Cutting board
Whole chicken

METHOD

1. Work through all the steps above for jointing a chicken into 6 pieces (left).

2. Cut each breast in half diagonally to make 8 pieces. One half of each breast will have the wing attached.

97 CARVING A ROAST CHICKEN

If there is one meat skill that every home cook should learn, it is how to carve a roast chicken. The correct technique will ensure that all the meat is removed from the carcass and waste is minimized. By carving the chicken before serving, it is easier to offer people a selection of white and dark meat.

TOOLS AND INGREDIENTS

Carving fork
Carving knife
Cutting board
Whole roast chicken

EXPERT TIPS

* A large, sharp knife is essential to cut neat, even slices.

METHOD

1. After allowing the cooked chicken to rest, put it on a clean cutting board.

2. Use a carving fork to steady the chicken with one hand. Using a carving knife, remove the legs by slicing down through the joint where the legs join the body.

3. Next, carve slices from the breasts by slicing evenly in a parallel motion along the rib cage of the bird. You can cut large slices or thinner slices, depending on preference. Alternatively, you can remove the breasts whole.

4. Remove the wings by cutting at the joints where they join the bird. You can remove the tips of the wings if preferred.

98 SCORING A DUCK BREAST

Duck has a thick layer of fat between the skin and the meat and scoring through the skin releases some of this fat, helping to create a crispy skin and reducing the amount of fat in the cooked duck.

METHOD

1 Put the duck breast on a board, skin side up.

2 Using a sharp paring knife, score a diagonal pattern across the skin without cutting through completely to the flesh underneath.

EXPERT TIPS

* Duck fat has a number of culinary uses so keep the fat that is rendered off the duck breasts when they cook. Like goose fat, duck fat is perfect for roasting potatoes. It can also be used for frying and adding extra flavor to dishes like casseroles and soups. Alternatively, try making duck confit – where meat is cooked very slowly in fat until it is very tender and literally falls off the bone.

TOOLS AND INGREDIENTS

Sharp paring knife
Cutting board
Duck breast

99 SEARING A DUCK BREAST

Searing is a cooking technique that lightly cooks the ingredient. It is widely used for cooking steak, duck and fish such as tuna steaks.

TOOLS AND INGREDIENTS

Heavy based skillet
Sharp chef's knife or
  paring knife

Cutting board
Duck breast
Salt and pepper

EXPERT TIPS

* Make sure the skillet is very hot before adding the duck. Searing is used to help crisp up the skin.

* Searing will result in rare meat – if you like your meat well done, cook for longer. You can either continue cooking in the skillet, or transfer the duck to the oven to roast.

METHOD

1. Heat a heavy based skillet until it's very hot.

2. Meanwhile, pat the duck breast dry using paper towels, to remove excess moisture, then season with salt and pepper. Using a sharp chef's knife or paring knife, score the skin of the duck breast in a crosshatch pattern (see opposite).

3. When the skillet is hot enough, put the duck breast in the skillet, skin side down.

4. As the duck begins to sear, you will see the fat melt away. Continue cooking for 3-4 minutes then lift the skillet to check the skin. It should be crisp and golden; continue for a few more minutes if needed.

5. Turn the duck breast over and cook for a further 3-5 minutes.

SEAFOOD SKILLS

We are constantly told about the huge health benefits that come from regularly eating fish. With such a wide variety of fresh fish and shellfish available from specialty stores, supermarkets and – if you are lucky – direct from fishing boats, there is no excuse not to prepare this delicious and nutritious food.

From stews, soups, risottos and paellas, to salt-baked, broiled, seared and the classic battered fish dinner, this versatile ingredient should regularly feature on the menu. Of course, there are increasing concerns about diminishing stocks of certain fish varieties and – as consumers – we should ensure our fish is caught sustainably. However, by steering clear of over-fished varieties and buying carefully we can enjoy the oceans' harvest whenever we choose.

This chapter will guide fish and shellfish novices through the basics of scaling and gutting fish, preparing shellfish and mastering some basic cooking techniques.

100 IDENTIFYING AND CHOOSING FISH

If you are used to buying your fish neatly chopped into fillets and sealed in plastic packaging, then it is definitely time to venture into a specialty store or market and buy whole, fresh fish that you can take home and prepare yourself. Use your senses to guide you to the freshest fish: eyes should be bright, clear and bulging; gills should be bright, clean and red; the body should be firm, smooth and stiff; and the skin should be shiny and damp. Any natural markings or colorings on the fish should be bright and obvious.

Round fish should have firm and meaty flesh. They are ideal for baking, broiling, barbecuing, pan-frying, braising and stewing. The flesh combines well with many other ingredients and can be cooked with strong flavorings. Species include bass, bream, catfish, cod, eel, haddock, hake, mackerel, monkfish, mullet, salmon, trout, snapper, swordfish and tuna.

Flat fish have a delicate flesh and texture. The fillets have fewer bones than round fish. They are ideal for baking, steaming, poaching and pan-frying. Species include brill, sole, grouper, halibut, john dory, plaice, ray, skate and turbot.

Fish

Cod
- Versatile. Broil, fry, poach, bake or add to stews.

Eel
- Braise, poach, bake or hot-smoke. Remove the skin before eating.

Haddock
- Deep-fry in batter, pan-fry broil, poach, bake or add to stews.

Hake
- Bake, broil, fry, poach or steam.

Monkfish
- Broil, bake, roast, fry or barbecue. Remove the membrane covering the flesh before cooking.

Salmon
- Poach, fry, broil, hot- and cold-smoke, use in mousses, pies, fishcakes and stews.

Sardines
- Broil.

Trout
- Fry, broil, bake, hot-smoke or griddle.

Snapper
- Pan-fry, broil, bake or steam the whole fish. Pan-fry, broil or steam fillets.

Swordfish
- Pan-fry, broil, bake or use cubed to make kebabs.

Sea Bass
- Pan-fry, broil, bake, steam or poach.

Tuna
- Pan-fry, broil, barbecue or serve raw as sushi or sashimi. Avoid baking.

Grouper
- Fry, broil or use in soups and stews. Remove the skin before eating.

Halibut
- Bake, braise or poach.

Turbot
- Bake or poach the whole fish. Broil pan-fry, poach or steam fillets.

Skate
- Pan-fry, deep-fry, bake or poach.

101 SCALING

Although not difficult, this can be a very messy job so it is best to work in a sink when scaling fish. If you have never tried this before, it might take a couple of attempts to perfect the technique but it is the best way to enjoy the freshest fish at home.

TOOLS AND INGREDIENTS

Cutting board
Large chef's knife
Fish (depending on recipe)

METHOD

1. Put the fish on a board (ideally in the sink so that the scales don't spread around too much) with the head facing away from you.

2. Hold the fish firmly by the tail. Using a large chef's knife, scrape the scales away with the back of the knife, moving from the tail down toward the head.

3. Turn the fish over and repeat on the other side until all the scales have been removed.

4. Rinse the fish thoroughly under cold running water to clean it, and then pat dry with paper towels.

EXPERT TIPS

* If you want to avoid the mess, put the fish inside a large plastic bag and work inside that. If you leave the bag fully open at the top you will be able to see what you are doing but all the mess will remain in the bag and can be easily disposed of afterward.

* Although the scales are tough, the flesh of the fish is soft so don't press down too firmly when removing the scales or you might damage the fish.

* You can buy specialty fish scaling utensils but a knife or even a spoon will get the job done equally well.

* Take the time to remove all the scales — paying attention to the more inaccessible parts, such as the fins and tail, and around the head.

102 CLEANING A ROUND FISH

As with scaling, this job is best done over a sink, as it can be messy. Different varieties of fish require different preparation techniques; flat and round fish need to be treated very differently when gutting and filleting.

TOOLS AND INGREDIENTS

Kitchen shears or sharp
 chef's knife
Tablespoon
Fish

EXPERT TIPS

* If you are not cooking the fish immediately, pack it into some ice to keep it really chilled and fresh until you are ready to cook it.

* Fish is always best gutted when fresh – so get this messy job out of the way before freezing your fish.

METHOD

1. Hold the fish firmly in one hand, stomach side up.

2. Using kitchen shears or a sharp chef's knife, cut along the length of the fish, starting at the tail end and stopping just below the head, at the gills.

3. Using your hands (this is the messy part), pull out all the innards and discard.

4. Use a tablespoon to run along the spine of the fish removing any remaining guts and blood vessels – it is important to ensure that everything is removed before cooking.

5. Rinse the fish thoroughly under cold, running water.

103 BONING A ROUND FISH

Round fish can be prepared as steaks, with the bone left in, but often a recipe will call for the bone to be removed – this skill will show you how.

TOOLS AND INGREDIENTS

Flexible fillet knife   Tweezers
Kitchen shears   Fish
Cutting board

METHOD

1. Hold the cleaned fish (see opposite), stomach side up, on a cutting board. Using a sharp, flexible fillet knife, run the blade of the knife along one side of the backbone.

2. Repeat on the other side, taking care not to cut all the way through the flesh.

3. Now use kitchen shears to cut under and around the bone and remove it.

4. Run your fingers along the inside of the fish to feel for any small pin bones, and remove these with scissors.

5. Rinse the boned fish under cold, running water and check once more for any missed bones.

104 SKINNING A ROUND FISH

If you are preparing fish for a stir-fry or curry you may wish to remove the skin.

TOOLS AND INGREDIENTS

Kitchen knife
Cutting board
Fish

METHOD

1. Hold the fish skin side down on a cutting board. Using a kitchen knife and working away from you, push the blade of the knife between the skin and the flesh.

2. Work along the piece of fish until all the skin has come away.

EXPERT TIPS

* Keep a small pile of salt on the cutting board and rub it onto your fingers from time to time to help you to get a better grip.

105 FILLETING A ROUND FISH

Round fish produce nice plump fillets that work well with a number of different cooking techniques. Fish with firmer flesh – such as salmon or monkfish – can handle longer cooking times in recipes such as curries or fish stews. Delicate fish can also be used in these dishes; simply place on top of the other ingredients for the last few minutes of cooking time. If a lid is placed over the pot, the fillets will gently steam.

METHOD

1. Put the scaled (see page 126) and cleaned (see page 128) fish on a cutting board. Using a flexible fillet knife, cut along the base of the head on one side of the fish.

2. Now cut down from the head, along the backbone, keeping the knife blade as flat and as close to the bone as possible. The fillet should be sliced off completely at the tail end.

3. Repeat on the other side so that you have two neat fillets of the same size. Trim the excess skin away from the fillets and neaten the edges.

4. Use clean tweezers to remove the bones from the fillets.

TOOLS AND INGREDIENTS

Flexible fillet knife
Cutting board
Tweezers

Fish (depending on recipe)

EXPERT TIPS

* If you prefer, you can remove the head completely before making the fillets – simply cut the whole way through it at the first step.

106 FILLETING A FLAT FISH

As the backbone is located centrally on a flat fish when it is laid on a cutting board, a different technique is required when it comes to filleting these varieties.

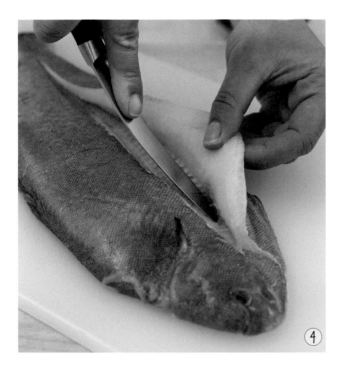

(4)

TOOLS AND INGREDIENTS

Cutting board
Sharp fillet knife

Fish (depending on recipe)

EXPERT TIPS

* Flat fish fillets are thin so it is important to work as close to the bone as possible to minimize waste.

METHOD

1. Put the fish on a large board with the dark side facing up.

2. Using a sharp fillet knife, run the blade along the outside edge of the fish, at the point at which the flesh meets the fins.

3. Now cut along the center of the fish, starting at the head and working down to the tail.

4. Start on one side, and cut the fillet away from the center of the fish using small, even strokes with the knife. Try to keep as close to the bone as possible so that none of the flesh is wasted.

5. Turn the fish around to repeat on the other side so that you have two fillets of the same size.

6. Now turn the fish over and cut around the head. Repeat the filleting process from Step 3.

107 OVEN POACHING

Poaching makes the most of the subtle flavor and delicate flesh of fish. The liquid helps to keep the fish moist while cooking in the oven, as it basically steams in the juices and soaks up the flavors from the liquid.

TOOLS AND INGREDIENTS

Roasting pan
Aluminum foil

Poaching liquid (see
    expert tips)
Fish (according to recipe)

METHOD

1. Line a suitable size roasting pan with foil (make sure there's enough length to completely cover and seal the fish).

2. Put the fish in the center of the foil in the pan and pull up the sides of the foil to create an open parcel around the fish.

3. Pour over the required amount of poaching liquid (see expert tips).

4. Pull the foil parcel around the fish and seal it by turning over the ends tightly at the top and around the sides.

5. Bake in the oven for the required time.

EXPERT TIPS

* Poaching liquids vary according to recipes; however, you can create your own liquid according to preference. You don't need a lot — just enough to cover the bottom of the foil — as the steam produced will cook the fish. Try a dash of white wine, olive oil and a few squeezes of lemon juice for a fresh, zesty flavor. Scatter in some freshly chopped herbs such as dill or parsley, and a little chopped garlic for even more flavor.

* If you want a bolder sauce, add spices, chopped chili and some chopped fresh ginger to the poaching liquid.

* After cooking, the poaching liquid can be reduced (simmered until it is concentrated) in a pan and you can use it as a sauce — add a tablespoon of heavy cream to create a richer sauce.

108 POACHING IN A FISH POACHER

Fish poacher pans are specifically designed to poach fish to perfection. The shape allows the fish room but also keeps it compact so that it cooks evenly and the steam is retained.

TOOLS AND INGREDIENTS

Fish poacher pan
Fish (according to recipe)
Poaching liquid (see
  expert tip, opposite)

METHOD

1 Put the fish on the rack of the pan and place inside the poacher pan.

2 Pour over the required amount of poaching liquid (see expert tip, opposite) You will need more poaching liquid in a fish poacher pan than you do for oven poaching, so adjust the amounts accordingly – the liquid should half cover the fish.

3 Cover the poacher pan with the lid and cook for the required time.

EXPERT TIPS

* It is easy to overcook fish so keep a close eye on timings and adjust accordingly for small fish or fillets. A minute too long could be the difference between succulent, flaky fish and dry, overcooked fish.

109 OVEN BAKING IN FOIL

As with poaching in the oven, this method uses aluminum foil to create a parcel around the fish so that it remains moist.

TOOLS AND INGREDIENTS

Large roasting pan
Aluminum foil
Fish (according to recipe)
Flavorings (according to
recipe, or see expert tip)

METHOD

1. Line a large flat roasting pan with foil, allowing enough excess on each side to be able to seal the fish completely in a parcel.

2. Put the fish in the center of the foil on the roasting pan and add your chosen seasonings and flavorings (or follow amounts in the recipe).

3. Seal with the excess foil, so that you have a neat parcel but there is room around the fish for the steam to circulate.

4. Bake in the oven for the required cooking time.

EXPERT TIPS

* A drizzle of olive oil, some salt and pepper, a few slices of lemon and some finely chopped garlic and shallots will add flavor to the finished fish, without detracting from its natural, subtle flavor. You can also add fresh herbs or spices, depending on the style of dish you are cooking and how much extra flavor you require.

110 BAKING EN PAPILLOTE

You may have seen a beautiful package of fragrant fish presented to you in paper at a restaurant but this technique works equally well at home and it isn't half as complicated as it looks.

TOOLS AND INGREDIENTS

Parchment paper
Pencil
Kitchen shears
Baking sheet

Fish (according to recipe)
Seasonings and flavorings
  (according to recipe)

METHOD

1. On parchment paper, draw a heart shape that is larger than the piece of fish you are cooking, and cut it out.

2. Put the fish on one half of the heart with the seasonings and flavorings (according to recipe, or use a splash of olive oil, white wine, a minced garlic clove and a squeeze of lemon juice).

3. Fold the other half of the paper over the fish and seal all the edges by folding the paper over and twisting the bottom point. It needs to be well secured to ensure the liquid doesn't escape and the fish can steam and remain moist during cooking.

4. Put the paper parcel on a baking sheet and bake in the oven for the required time.

111 STEAMING

This technique is ideal for delicate fish fillets, or for whole fish that require gentle cooking.

TOOLS AND INGREDIENTS

Steamer, or cooking pot
with steamer insert
Cooking liquid (according
to recipe)

Fish (according to recipe)

EXPERT TIPS

* If you don't have a steamer, you can use a stainless
steel strainer with the lid of the pot on top of it.

METHOD

1 In a steamer, or a cooking pot that has a
steamer insert, heat your chosen liquid. This
could be broth, water, wine or a combination
of ingredients.

2 When the liquid has begun to simmer, put
the fish in the steamer, and put the steamer
inside the pot. Cover and steam for the
required time. The liquid shouldn't reach
the fish; it should simmer underneath it, so
that the fish is cooked entirely by the steam
– remaining moist but not soaked in liquid.

112 BAMBOO STEAMING

This technique is often used in Asian recipes.

TOOLS AND INGREDIENTS

Wok
Bamboo steamer
Steaming liquid (according
to recipe)

Flavorings (according to
recipe)
Fish

METHOD

1 Fill a wok halfway with your chosen liquid
and flavorings (this could be broth, rice wine,
ginger, garlic, chili – or a combination).

2 Put the fish in a bamboo steamer, cover with
the lid and then put the steamer in the wok.
Steam for the required time.

113 BROILING

Broiled fish takes on a subtle smoky flavor and is delicious served with piquant sauces.

TOOLS AND INGREDIENTS

Fish (whole)

METHOD

1. Heat the broiler in the oven to medium-high.

2. When it is hot, put the fish on the broiler rack and place under the broiler.

3. Cooking times will vary depending on the size and variety of fish but as a rough guide, you should cook the fish for 2–3 minutes (longer for larger fish) on each side.

4. Remove when the flesh is cooked through and the skin is crispy.

114 BARBECUING

The flavor of the barbecued fish and any marinade mingles with the smoke from the coals.

TOOLS AND INGREDIENTS

Fish grilling basket
Fish (whole)
Salt and pepper
Flavorings (according to
  recipe or taste)

METHOD

1. Season the fish generously with salt and pepper then put on a fish grilling basket. You can add flavorings to the fish cavity, either according to the recipe or personal taste – e.g., slices of garlic and lemon, sprigs of rosemary or thyme or chopped chili.

2. Close the fish basket and cook the fish on a hot barbecue for approximately 3 minutes on each side (larger fish will take longer and barbecues will vary so always ensure the fish is fully cooked).

3. When cooked, the flesh should come away with a fork and the skin should be crispy.

115 BAKING IN A SALT CRUST

Far from creating an overly salty finished dish, this method of cooking gently bakes the fish in a sealed cocoon of salt. This ensures that all the flavor is retained and the fish cooks evenly, resulting in delicate, mouth-watering flesh. The fish steams in its own juices so none of the moisture is lost.

TOOLS AND INGREDIENTS

Heavy-based pot or
 ovenproof dish
Small hammer
Sea salt (approximately
 2¼ lb/1 kg)
Water to sprinkle
Fish (whole, such as sea
 bass)

METHOD

1. Cover the base of a heavy-based pot or ovenproof dish with an even layer of sea salt.

2. Put the fish on top and cover it with the remaining sea salt (this should be a fairly compact, thick layer).

3. Sprinkle the top of the salt crust lightly with water and bake in a hot oven at 400°F (200°C) for about 40 minutes.

4. Once cooked, carefully crack away the salt crust with a small hammer (alternatively, you can use a knife to cut off the top of the crust).

5. Carefully remove the fish and serve whole, or cut into fillets. If you want to really impress your guests, take the whole dish to the table and remove the fish from its salty bed just before serving.

* You can use this technique with other food such as game, poultry and root vegetables.

* If the crust is well compacted, you can cook the fish on barbecue coals for the same result.

* For extra flavor, try infusing the salt with herbs or citrus peel.

116 IDENTIFYING AND CHOOSING SHELLFISH

This section will cover creatures with tough shells, such as crabs and clams, as well as soft-bodied water-dwellers including octopus and squid. They include some of the world's most expensive gourmet foods such as oysters and lobster. The majority benefit from simple cooking techniques such as broiling or steaming or may be eaten raw.

Lobster and crab. When buying live these should be active and heavy. If cooked, the shell should be undamaged. They should smell fresh, and should not have strong "fishy" odor.

Mussels and clams should not be open or cracked. If are too dirty or covered in barnacles, avoid them.

Scallops are normally sold already opened. The flesh should be translucent and have a slight gray color (not too white). They should have fresh sweet smell, not a strong odor.

Oysters should be tightly closed and the shell should not be damaged. It is best to eat and buy them during months that have the letter "R" in them.

Shrimp, langoustine and so on should be firm with shells that are shiny and gray if raw. Black spots are a sign of aging so avoid these.

Shellfish

Clams
- Steam, fry, boil, bake or eat raw depending on the species.

Crab
- Deep-fry, salads, seafood cocktails, and crab cakes depending on the species.

Mussels
- Steam, add to soups, stews and risottos, stuff and broil the half shells, add to pies and paellas.

Langoustine
- Only the tail meat is eaten. Also known as Dublin Bay prawns and scampi.

Crayfish
- Poach, often cooked with spices for a "crawfish boil" in the US.

Lobster
- Poach. The flesh may be served in the shell with a sauce.

Squid
- Deep-fry, pan-fry or use in soups, stews and paellas. Over-cooking can make it rubbery.

Oyster
- Serve raw; steam, coat in batter and deep-fry; or add to soups and stews.

Octopus
- Deep-fry, pan-fry or use in soups, stews and paellas. Over-cooking can make it rubbery.

Tiger Shrimp
- Poach, broil, or use in seafood cocktails, salads, paellas and stews. Attractive garnish with the shell on.

Shrimp
- Poach, broil, or use in seafood cocktails, salads, paellas and stews.

117 PEELING SHRIMP

It is so much more satisfying to peel your own shrimp than to buy bags of prepared seafood.

TOOLS AND INGREDIENTS

Shrimp

METHOD

1 Hold the shrimp firmly between your thumb and index finger, at the tail end.

2 Peel the whole shell off by pulling it away with your fingers. You can either leave the tail peeled or unpeeled.

3 If the head is attached to the shrimp, pull this off before peeling the rest of the shrimp. It should come away easily.

EXPERT TIPS

* If you are peeling the shrimp to serve to guests, leave the tail on: this is handy to hold onto if the shrimp are being dipped into a sauce, and it also makes the shrimp look nicer when presented at the table.

* Save the heads and skins to make a shellfish broth. Simply fry them in a little oil with some garlic and herbs then add water and a dash of white wine and simmer for 5-10 minutes for a quick and easy broth.

118 DEVEINING SHRIMP

The black line that runs along the back of the shrimp is the intestinal tract and the black color means that it's full. Although this doesn't sound particularly appetizing, it won't harm you if you eat it but removing it does improve the flavor and the appearance of the shrimp.

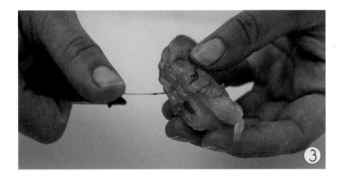

TOOLS AND INGREDIENTS

Sharp chef's knife

Shrimp (peeled, see opposite)

METHOD

1. Hold the peeled shrimp between your thumb and index finger.

2. With a small sharp chef's knife, score along the curved back of the shrimp to make a shallow incision.

3. Using the tip of the knife, lift out and remove the dark vein that runs along the center of the shrimp.

4. Rinse the shrimp under cold, running water before using.

119 KEEPING SHRIMP STRAIGHT FOR COOKING

Shrimp tend to curl up when they come into contact with heat so if you need straight shrimp for your recipe, here's the technique to follow. Remove the toothpick before serving.

TOOLS AND INGREDIENTS

Toothpick
Shrimp (peeled, see opposite)

METHOD

1. Once you have peeled the shrimp (see opposite), keep it straight and push a long toothpick down the center of the shrimp to prevent it from curling when it cooks.

120 COOKING CRAB

Freshly cooked crab is an affordable luxury and is surprisingly easy to prepare. They require no preparation before being put in the pot – all the tricky work is saved for later on, when it comes to cracking the crab and picking out the meat (see page 146).

TOOLS AND INGREDIENTS

Kitchen twine
Large pot with lid
Slotted spoon
Crab

METHOD

1. Use kitchen twine to tie the crab so that it remains compact in the pot. Pass the twine around the center of the crab, making sure the claws are snug against the main body.

2. Bring a large pot of water to a boil, then add salt. When the water is boiling, drop the crab into the pot and cover.

3. Cook for 15 minutes for the first 1 lb (450 g) of its weight, then an additional 2 minutes for each 4 oz (110 g) in excess of this.

4. When cooked, lift the crab out of the pot of liquid with a large slotted spoon. Rinse under cold, running water and leave to cool before cracking and picking out the meat.

EXPERT TIPS

* If you are cooking more than one crab, make sure you use a pot that is large enough to accommodate the crabs. Wait for the water to come back up to a boil after adding one crab and before adding the next crab to the pot.

* Add plenty of salt to the cooking water, 4 teaspoons (20 ml) is ideal.

* Once the crab has cooled, it can be stored, covered, in the refrigerator for up to 4 days.

* Whole cooked crabs can also be frozen. Put them in freezer bags and they will store safely for up to 3 months.

121 CRACKING CRAB

It is possible to buy prepared crab but if this is a favorite ingredient, there will come a time when you want to prepare and cook crabs from scratch. The technique is a bit tricky but that's not to say it's difficult – a little practice is all it takes.

TOOLS AND INGREDIENTS

Cutting board
Wooden rolling pin or
  crab crackers
Spoon

Sharp chef's knife
Pick or skewer
Crab (cooked)

METHOD

1. Put the cooked crab on a board, with the smooth side of the shell facing downward.

2. To remove the legs and claws, hold the body of the crab firmly and twist and pull the legs and claws backward and forward to detach them.

3. Using the wooden rolling pin or crab crackers, crack the claws around the middle, using the crackers. You should be able to slide the meat out in large pieces using a pick or skewer.

4. Next, remove the pointed tail by snapping it firmly away from the body.

5. The main shell of the body is broken by pressing down firmly with your thumbs onto the shell. You should be able to lift out the main section of meat — use a spoon to scrape out the brown meat.

6. Throw away the dead man's fingers (the gray gills) and any other debris.

7. With a sharp chef's knife, cut the body in half lengthwise and scrape out the white meat with a pick or skewer.

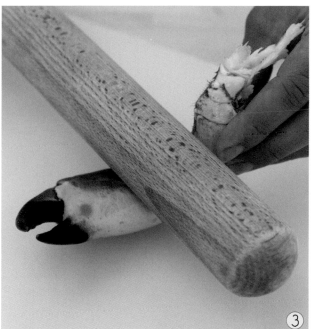

③

⑦

④

EXPERT TIPS

* If you prefer you can use a small mallet to crack the shell.

* If you find the shell is slippery, use a clean dish towel to get a grip on the crab as you work.

* Once you have picked all the meat from the crab, check through it carefully with your fingers to make sure there are no small pieces of shell remaining.

* The white crab meat is fine and delicate while the brown is rich and full flavored.

* You can serve the meat in the cleaned shell.

122 COOKING LOBSTER

This expensive ingredient needs to be cooked and prepared with care as it is generally saved for special occasions. If you have shied away from buying and cooking live lobsters in the past, you will discover that cooking one simply involves bringing a pot of water to a boil and keeping track of the time.

TOOLS AND INGREDIENTS

Large pot with lid
Slotted spoon
Lobster
4 tsp (20 ml) salt

EXPERT TIPS

* Live lobsters are best cooked and eaten as soon as possible.

METHOD

1. If you are cooking a live lobster, make sure the lobster's claws are tied with rubber bands before handling. Before you begin, weigh the lobster to calculate the cooking time (see below).

2. Bring a large pot of water to a boil.

3. When the water is boiling, add 4 teaspoons (20 ml) salt, then gently put the lobster into the liquid head first.

4. Bring back to a boil and cook the lobster for about 15 minutes if it weighs up to 1 lb (450 g). Add an extra 10 minutes of cooking time for each additional 1 lb (450 g) of weight. Once the shell is red, the lobster is cooked.

5. Remove the lobster from the pot with a large slotted spoon and leave to cool.

123 REMOVING MEAT FROM LOBSTER

As with crab, cracking and picking the meat from a lobster is a tricky job and will take patience and perseverance the first time you attempt it. However, once you have worked through the steps a couple of times, you will get much quicker at it.

TOOLS AND INGREDIENTS

Kitchen shears or sharp
 chef's knife
Crab crackers

Spoon
Cooked lobster

EXPERT TIPS

* If you clean out the shells, you can make dressed lobster: combining the lobster meat with sauce or simply placing it back in the shell before serving.

METHOD

1. Take the cooled, cooked lobster and cut along the length of the underside (kitchen shears are best for this, but a sharp chef's knife can also be used). Then cut along both sides of the tail.

2. Peel the tail shell back to expose the meat and gently pull the tail meat out, trying to keep it in a whole piece.

3. Next, cut the lobster in half using kitchen shears and crack the claws using crab crackers (see pages 146–147) to remove the meat.

4. With a spoon, remove the liver, stomach sac and the gills and discard them.

5. Once all the meat has been removed, check through it with your fingers to ensure that no small pieces of shell remain in the meat.

124 CLEANING MUSSELS AND CLAMS

As mussels and clams are often served in the shell, it is important to clean them up before cooking them.

TOOLS AND INGREDIENTS

Small, sharp chef's knife
Wire brush or scrubbing
  brush
Bowl
Mussels or clams

EXPERT TIPS

* The beard is the thin brown tuft that hangs out from the mussel, which it uses to attach itself to rocks or other surfaces. If you can't remove it by pulling it with your fingers, you can cut it off with kitchen shears.

* Mussels should be cooked within three days of being caught. Cooked mussels can be stored in the refrigerator for up to three days.

METHOD

1. With the back of a small, sharp chef's knife, scrape off any barnacles from the shells of the mussels. These should come away easily with a firm press of the knife.

2. Use your fingers to pull out any loose hairs (beards) by tugging them away firmly from the hinge end of the mussel.

3. Use a clean wire brush or stiff scrubbing brush to clean the mussels thoroughly under cold running water. Discard any mussels or clams that have broken or cracked shells. Do the same if they don't close when tapped gently on a surface.

4. Transfer the mussels or clams to a large bowl of cold water until needed.

125 STEAMING MUSSELS AND CLAMS

TOOLS AND INGREDIENTS

Large shallow pot with lid
Slotted spoon
Cooking liquid (according
   to recipe or see expert tip
   below)
Mussels or clams

EXPERT TIPS

* For 4 lbs (1.75 kg) of mussels, here is a simple cooking suggestion: fry 1 chopped shallot and 1 garlic clove in a little olive oil in the pot you will use to steam the mussels. Add 1 glass of white wine, bring to a boil then add the mussels to the pot and cover with the lid. The mussels are ready when they are all open (discard any that do not open). Just before the end of the cooking time, add a handful of chopped parsley.

METHOD

1. Put the cooking liquid (according to recipe or see expert tip below) in a large shallow pot with a lid and heat.

2. Once the liquid is hot, add the mussels or clams to the pot and cook, covered, over a high heat.

3. Shake the pot several times and check after 5 minutes. If the mussels or clams aren't all open, cover with the lid and continue to steam for a couple more minutes.

4. Once cooked, remove the mussels or clams from the cooking liquid with a slotted spoon and reduce the liquid slightly by simmering.

5. Discard any that are not opened and serve with the reduced cooking liquid as a sauce.

126 PREPARING OYSTERS

This is called shucking an oyster. It takes a bit of brute force but this isn't a difficult skill to master.

TOOLS AND INGREDIENTS

Dish towel   Oysters
Oyster knife

METHOD

1. Hold the oyster firmly in a folded dish towel
   with the round side of the shell down. Leave
   the peaked end (it looks like a hinge) of the
   oyster exposed and hold the other end inside
   the dish towel in the palm of your hand.

2. Push the oyster knife into the shell at the
   peaked end and slide the knife up and down
   the length of the shell to loosen both sides.

3. Once the shell sides are starting to loosen,
   twist the knife more vigorously to completely
   separate the shells at the hinge.

4. Carefully scrape along the top shell so that
   the oyster falls into the bottom half and
   then cut through the muscle at the hinge to
   completely separate the two shells. Check
   the oyster to make sure there are no shell
   fragments on it.

5. Loosen the edges around the oyster and
   serve.

127 OPENING AND PREPARING SCALLOPS

This has to be one of the prettiest shellfish you can buy, with its distinctive scalloped shell. It is also one of the most delicious and preparing your own scallops at home allows you to serve them exactly the way you want to.

TOOLS AND INGREDIENTS

Oyster knife
Spoon
Scallops

EXPERT TIPS

* The shells are so pretty that they can be used as serving plates (albeit small ones). Once you have cooked the scallops, sit them back in their shell halves and serve – either with a sauce or simply a squeeze of lemon juice or olive oil and a sprinkling of freshly chopped herbs.

METHOD

1. Hold the scallop with the round side fitted into the palm of your hand.

2. Repeat steps 2 to 4 from the previous skill (Preparing Oysters, opposite).

3. Remove the scallop from the muscle it sits on by using a spoon to scoop it out.

4. Detach the dark organs by pulling them off with your fingers. Make sure you don't remove the orange coral.

5. Remove the small white muscle from the side of the scallop.

6. At this point you can remove the coral if you don't wish to use it.

7. Rinse the scallop under cold, running water and it is now ready to cook.

128 PREPARING SQUID

This is another messy job so it's a good idea to prepare the squid over a large bowl or in the sink. If fresh squid evokes vacation memories, you can recreate them whenever you like once you have perfected this handy skill.

TOOLS AND INGREDIENTS

Chef's knife
Cutting board
Squid

METHOD

1. Hold the squid with a firm grip in one hand, with the head and tentacles nearest to you.

2. Use your fingers to pull the head and tentacles out of the body, by pulling firmly toward you.

3. Running along one side of the body of the squid is a large flat piece of cartilage, known as the pen – pull this out and discard.

4. With your fingers, pull off the thin purple lining of skin that covers the outside of the squid.

5. Next, cut the fins away from the body using a sharp chef's knife.

6. Separate the tentacles from the head by cutting them and pull out the sharp beak. Cut off the eyes and the mouth.

7. Rinse the body of the squid and the tentacles thoroughly under cold, running water.

8. You can leave the body whole, slice it into rings, or cut it open to form a flat piece, which you then score with a crosshatch pattern.

9. Pat the squid dry before cooking to remove any excess moisture.

(3)

EXPERT TIPS

* Squid needs to be cooked very quickly (2–3 minutes) as it tends to go rubbery and chewy if pan-fried for too long. However, it can handle long, slow cooking times, as it will tenderize again.

* When it comes to cooking, keep things simple: heat a little oil and chopped garlic in a skillet until hot, fry the squid for a couple of minutes then serve with a squeeze of lemon juice. Add a sprinkle of freshly chopped red chili to the cooking pan if you want a bit of heat in the finished dish.

EGG SKILLS

Eggs are delicious, nutritious and economical. They can be served in some form at every meal from breakfast to dinner, and from appetizer through to dessert (and used in plenty of cakes and sweet treats in between). This staple ingredient is one of the most essential in the kitchen yet its preparation can often be a daunting prospect for kitchen novices. So, if the thought of poaching an egg fills you with dread, or you still suffer nightmares from a disastrous soufflé attempt at a dinner party, read on.

This chapter includes everything you need to know about this most simple yet versatile ingredient. We cover basic techniques through to the more challenging and provide all the tips for safe and delicious cooking.

129 CRACKING AN EGG

Anyone who has to fend for themselves in the kitchen needs to be able to crack an egg. Get it right and the egg will fall smoothly and intact into the bowl; get it wrong and sticky egg white will douse the surfaces, and the egg that makes it to the bowl will be full of tiny pieces of shell. Below are some tried and tested techniques for getting it right every time.

TOOLS AND INGREDIENTS

Bowl or glass
Knife or spoon
Eggs

METHODS

1. Crack the egg onto the edge of a bowl or a glass to break the shell. Pull the shell apart, allowing the egg to fall into the bowl.

2. Crack the middle of the egg with the back of a knife or a spoon and pull apart to release the egg.

3. Crack two eggs together to break one.

130 TESTING EGGS FOR FRESHNESS

As eggs age they take in air and their texture becomes less firm. While this isn't a problem for most baking, if you want beautiful round poached eggs or fried eggs with a pert yolk rising from the white, then this technique helps you test which of your eggs are the freshest.

TOOLS AND INGREDIENTS

Tumbler or other large glass
Egg

METHOD

1. To test the freshness of an egg, put it in a glass of water: if it is fresh, it will rest on the bottom of the glass; an old, stale egg will float to the surface.

131 SEPARATING AN EGG YOLK AND EGG WHITE

Many recipes call for only the yolks or the whites of eggs to be used so this is a skill worth perfecting if you plan to do a lot of baking, and the best part is you don't need any fancy kitchen gadgets. Don't discard the unused part of the egg: yolks can be used to make fresh mayonnaise, while whites are perfect for meringues or omelets.

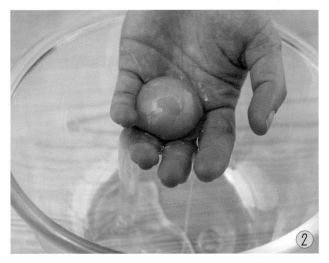

TOOLS AND INGREDIENTS

Bowl
Egg

METHOD (USING HANDS)

1. Crack the egg over a bowl (see opposite).

2. Cup one hand and pour the egg into it, allowing the white to pass through your fingers. The yolk should remain in your cupped palm.

METHOD (USING THE SHELL)

1. Crack the egg over a bowl (see opposite).

2. Tip the yolk back and forth between the two shell halves, allowing the white to fall into the bowl below.

EXPERT TIPS

* Spare yolks and whites will keep for 2-3 days if covered and kept in the refrigerator. Add a drop of water to yolks as they dry out otherwise. You can freeze egg whites in an ice tray to use another time.

132 MAKING AN EGG WASH

Egg washes are used to help attach pie crust lids and to brush over finished tarts and pies before cooking.

METHOD

1. Mix 1 egg yolk with 1 tablespoon (15 ml) water.

2. Beat well with a small whisk or fork until well combined.

EXPERT TIPS

* Use a pastry brush to create a neat layer of egg wash over pies and tarts.

TOOLS AND INGREDIENTS

Bowl
Small whisk or fork
1 tbsp (15 ml) water
Egg

133 BOILING EGGS

Nothing beats a perfectly cooked boiled egg complemented by a pile of buttery toast. It all comes down to timing so don't wander too far away from the pot.

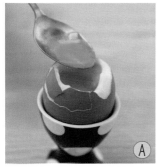

TOOLS AND INGREDIENTS

Pot
Slotted spoon
Eggs
Pinch of salt

EXPERT TIPS

* If chilled eggs come into contact with boiling water, they will probably crack on impact — always use room-temperature eggs.

* Don't let the water boil too rapidly or the eggs will knock against the side of the pot — or into each other — and they may crack.

METHOD A (SOFT BOILED)

1. Gently lower the required number of eggs into a pot of boiling water, using a slotted spoon. Add a pinch of salt.

2. Simmer the eggs gently for 3-4 minutes, the exact time will depend on what egg size you're cooking (smaller cooks more quickly) and just how runny you like them, and remove with a slotted spoon.

METHOD B (HARD BOILED)

1. Gently lower the required number of eggs into a pot of boiling water, using a slotted spoon. Add a pinch of salt.

2. Simmer the eggs gently for 6-10 minutes, as above, the exact time will depend on required firmness and egg size.

3. Remove from the water with a slotted spoon and immediately put into a bowl of cold water to prevent the yolks from discoloring.

134 POACHING EGGS

A lot of people shy away from poaching their own eggs – saving the pleasure for restaurants or hotels where chefs have perfected the art of cooking perfectly poached eggs every time. However follow this simple method and your breakfasts will be transformed.

TOOLS AND INGREDIENTS

Small pot
Small cup, glass or bowl
Wooden spoon

Slotted spoon
1 tbsp (15 ml) vinegar
Egg

EXPERT TIPS

* You can prepare poached eggs in advance: poach as above then transfer to a bowl filled with ice water so that the egg stops cooking. When you're ready to serve just lower the egg back into a pot of boiling water for 1 minute then drain and serve.

METHOD

1. Bring a small pot of water to a boil and add 1 tablespoon (15 ml) vinegar (wine vinegar or regular).

2. Crack the egg into a small cup, glass or bowl.

3. Stir the water vigorously with a wooden spoon until you have a whirlpool effect in the center. Reduce the heat.

4. Pour the egg into the center of the whirlpool and it will form itself into a round shape.

5. Remove with a slotted spoon after 3 minutes. Hold the egg in the spoon for a few seconds to allow the water to drain away.

135 BAKING EGGS

The perfect comfort food, a baked egg is simple and reassuring. Using a water-filled roasting pan to cook them spreads the heat evenly and cooks the eggs all the way through.

TOOLS AND INGREDIENTS

Ramekin or individual
  soufflé dish
Parchment paper
Aluminum foil
Deep roasting pan
Butter

Egg
2 tbsp (30 ml) heavy
  cream
Salt and pepper

METHOD

1. Butter a ramekin or soufflé dish and crack the egg into it.

2. Pour over 2 tablespoons (30 ml) heavy cream and season with salt and pepper.

3. Cover tightly with aluminum foil. Line the roasting pan with parchment paper and place the ramekin on top. Add water to come a third of the way up the ramekin.

4. Bake in an oven preheated to 350°F (180°C) for 6–8 minutes.

EXPERT TIPS

* If you have one, you can use a specialty bain-marie.

* Lining the pan with parchment paper helps to distribute the heat evenly.

136 MAKING A FRENCH OMELET FOR 1

When you're in need of a hearty meal from store cupboard ingredients, an omelet is the perfect solution. It's a simple skill to master and can be elaborated on with different fillings, such as cheese, ham or tomatoes sprinkled on before you fold it, or by adding fresh herbs to the mixture.

TOOLS AND INGREDIENTS

Bowl
Nonstick skillet
Whisk
Fork

2 eggs
Salt and pepper
1 tbsp (15 g) butter

METHOD

1. Crack 2 eggs into a bowl and season with salt and pepper. Beat the eggs with a whisk until combined.

2. Heat a small nonstick skillet and melt 1 tablespoon (15 g) butter in it.

3. Once the butter is foaming, pour in the beaten eggs and tilt the skillet so the eggs are evenly spread.

4. Using a fork, quickly pull the edges of the omelet in as it cooks.

5. Tilt the skillet to one side and gently flip one half onto the other. Cook for anther 30 seconds or so leaving the center soft and the outside firm.

137 WHISKING EGG WHITES

If meringues (see pages 190–191) are on the menu you need to be able to whisk egg whites to the correct consistency. There are two methods – one requires more muscle.

TOOLS AND INGREDIENTS

Stainless steel or glass
  bowl
Balloon whisk

Electric mixer (if
  machine beating)
Eggs

EXPERT TIPS

* Sometimes a pinch of salt can help to make whisking easier.

* Ensure that the bowl you use when whisking is scrupulously clean. The smallest amount of oil, grease or egg yolk will contaminate the eggs and they won't fluff up. This also applies to the whisk you are using.

METHOD (BY HAND)

1. Separate the egg yolks and egg whites. Set aside the yolks to use on another occasion and put the egg whites in a large stainless steel or glass bowl.

2. Using a large balloon whisk, beat the egg whites in big circular movements, lifting the whites upward from the base of the bowl.

3. Depending on your requirements, either whisk until the whites are holding soft peaks or continue until they are holding stiff peaks.

METHOD (BY MACHINE)

1. Put the egg whites in the bowl of an electric mixer.

2. Gradually increase the speed and beat until the whites are the required consistency.

138 SOUFFLÉ

Soufflés often strike fear into the heart of the home cook and the disappointment of a deflated soufflé at a dinner party means that many people only attempt them once. But fear not, help is at hand with this fail-safe technique to achieve perfect soufflés every time.

TOOLS AND INGREDIENTS

2 ramekins
Balloon whisk
Large metal spoon or
  spatula
3 bowls
Pot

3 tbsp (45 ml) butter,
  plus extra for greasing
2 tbsp (30 ml) cocoa
  powder
3 oz (75 g) semisweet
  chocolate
½ tsp (3 ml) vanilla
  extract
2 eggs
2 tbsp (30 ml) superfine
  sugar
Pinch of salt
Pinch of cream of tartar

METHOD

1. Line the ramekins by greasing the sides and base then coating them with 2 tablespoons (30 ml) cocoa. Tip out the excess.

2. Break 3 oz (75 g) chocolate into a bowl and add 3 tablespoons (45 ml) butter. Place the bowl over a pot of simmering water, and stir occasionally until it has melted. Remove from the heat and add ½ teaspoon vanilla extract.

3. Separate 2 eggs (see page 159) and whisk the yolks into the chocolate mixture one at a time until smooth. Set aside.

EXPERT TIPS

* Running your thumb around the edge of the mixture will help to produce a more pronounced rise and keep the rise neat although it's not essential.

* Some chefs cook their soufflés in a bain-marie which will help the heat spread evenly and produce a more uniform rise.

* You can prepare the recipe in advance up to step 7 and keep them covered in the refrigerator. Add an extra 5 minutes in the oven if cooking from chilled.

4. In a clean bowl, slowly add 2 tablespoons (30 ml) superfine sugar and a pinch each of salt and cream of tartar to the egg whites and whisk constantly until the mixture forms stiff peaks when you lift the whisk.

5. Using a spoon or spatula, gently fold the chocolate mixture into the egg whites.

6. Fold very gently until the mixture is uniform in color but be careful not to over-mix it.

7. Spoon into the ramekins so it is level with the top.

8. Bake the soufflés in a preheated oven 375°F (190°C) for 20 minutes.

9. Serve immediately before the soufflés begin to deflate.

PASTRY AND BAKING SKILLS

Baking is often considered to be the most scientific and technical of all the cooking skills. With this in mind, we have collected together the most important of the baking techniques – those that will see you through most recipes for bread, cakes, cookies, pies and tarts.

When it comes to baking, precision is definitely required, as is patience and confidence. It is a good idea to arm yourself with the right tools – investing in some specialty bakeware if necessary – and get to know your way around your equipment and oven.

Always begin a baking session with everything prepared and organized and keep a calm head. This means gathering together all the ingredients and utensils that the recipe requires and working methodically through each stage of the recipe, keeping track of all the processes and timings as you go.

139 MAKING BASIC PIE CRUST

A good pie crust is the pride of every home baker. True, you can buy prepared pie dough but it isn't as satisfying as making your own from scratch. It isn't difficult, you just need to set aside a little time to prepare then chill the crust.

TOOLS AND INGREDIENTS

Large mixing bowl
Fine strainer
Pastry blender (optional)
Fork
1½ cups (220 g) all-
  purpose flour
1 tsp (5 ml) salt

½ cup (1 stick or 110 g)
  butter
1 egg

METHOD

1. Sift the flour and salt through a fine strainer into a large mixing bowl.

2. Add the chilled, diced butter to the flour and, using your fingers or a pastry blender, "cut in" (see page 179) until you have a consistency resembling bread crumbs. Lift the crumbs up and out of the bowl as you work, to incorporate as much air as possible.

3. Add 1 beaten egg to the dry ingredients and bring together using a fork and then using your hands.

4. You may have to add 1–2 tablespoons (15–30 ml) chilled water if the dough doesn't come together. The water will add sufficient moisture for it to form a cohesive shape.

5. Mold the dough into a ball and then flatten into a disk shape. Wrap in plastic wrap or put in a food bag and chill in the refrigerator for at least 30 minutes, or until needed.

EXPERT TIPS

* Always use half the amount of butter to flour – work in either cups or grams, don't mix.

* Don't overwork the dough otherwise it will be tough. It is having the butter broken down into little chunks that makes pastry crumbly.

* Making pie dough on a cold surface is best – as is having cold hands.

* For sweet pie crust, add 1 tablespoon (15 ml) superfine sugar to the flour before sieving.

* For flaky pie crust, just add a little less water to the dough.

* You can also freeze the dough – keep it in an airtight container or freezer bag for up to three months.

140 PUFF PASTRY

Making your own puff pastry involves a lot of work. The ones you can buy from a store are very decent these days and won't have an impact on the taste or texture of your finished dish.

TOOLS AND INGREDIENTS

Rolling pin
Flour

Store-bought puff pastry

METHOD

1. Make sure your dough is chilled before you start.

2. Roll out and prepare the dough on a cold surface in a cool room. Marble or granite is best, if you have the option.

3. Try not to over-handle the dough, as once it starts to warm up it is harder to work with. If your hands tend to warm up easily, keep a bowl of ice water next to you and dip them in to cool them off while working.

4. Once the dough has been shaped and set into the dish for the recipe, chill it again before baking.

5. Make sure the oven has reached the right temperature before the dough goes in, otherwise it will lose its crispness.

141 LINING A PIE DISH

This skill will see you through a whole selection of pies and tarts – both savory and sweet.

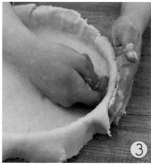

TOOLS AND INGREDIENTS

Rolling pin
Pie dish
Sharp chef's knife
(optional)

Flour
Prepared pie crust dough
(see page 170)

EXPERT TIPS

* Mend any tears by moistening a pastry scrap with water, sticking it over the gap and smoothing it in.

METHOD

1. Roll out the prepared dough into a large circular shape on a lightly floured surface. It is best to work from the center of the dough toward the edges to ensure an even layer. The dough must be larger than the pie dish.

2. Wrap the pastry loosely over the rolling pin and gently lay it over the dish, making sure there is enough dough to line the inside of the dish with excess hanging over the edges.

3. Using your knuckle, gently press the dough around and inside the dish until neatly lined.

4. Roll the rolling pin firmly over the top of the dish to remove the excess pastry. Alternatively, you can trim it with a small, sharp chef's knife.

5. To crimp the edges of the dough, use the index finger of one hand to make a dent in the crust, while the index finger and thumb of the other hand push the dough around it.

142 BLIND BAKING

Blind baking refers to baking the pastry for a pie or tart for a short time before the filling is added. This stops the crust from going soggy and ensures it is fully cooked and crumbly. Fillings will sometimes require less cooking time than the crust, so giving it a head start will ensure that the whole pie is cooked at the same time.

TOOLS AND INGREDIENTS

Fork
Parchment paper
Pie weights or dried
  beans
Pie crust-lined pie dish

EXPERT TIPS

* When pricking with a fork, don't puncture the dough too much or the filling will leak out of the shell.

METHOD

1. Prick the base of the dough-lined pie dish all over with a fork. This will stop the crust from blistering while it cooks.

2. Put a piece of parchment paper over the dish and fill it with either pie weights or any dried beans.

3. Bake at 350°F (180°C) for 10–15 minutes until the crust feels firm to the touch.

4. Remove the paper and pie weights from the pie and bake for a further 5 minutes, until the crust is a light golden color. Now you can add the filling to the pie crust and cook according to the recipe.

143 GREASING AND FLOURING A CAKE OR LOAF PAN

It is always best to use a springform cake pan when baking cakes or loaves – it is much easier to release the cake once it is cooked. Greasing the pan stops the cake from sticking to it by creating a nonstick layer between the pan and the contents.

METHOD

1. Remove 1 tablespoon (15 ml) butter from the refrigerator and allow it to reach room temperature. Alternatively, melt the butter.

2. Use parchment paper, or a pastry brush if you melted the butter, to spread the butter all over the inside of the cake pan. Make sure all surfaces are evenly coated: you can check this by holding the cake pan up to the light and checking for any areas that aren't shiny.

3. Now, sprinkle the surfaces with flour. Tip the pan around to make sure there is an even coating of flour all over it then tip out any excess.

TOOLS AND INGREDIENTS

Cake pan
1 tbsp (15 ml) butter
Flour

EXPERT TIPS

* You can also use a pastry brush to spread the flour around the inside of the pan. It can help to keep the mess levels down.

144 LINING A CAKE PAN

Don't despair over cakes stuck in pans. This technique will help your cakes glide effortlessly out.

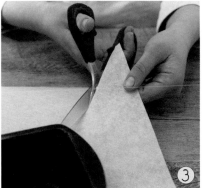

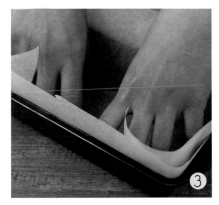

TOOLS AND INGREDIENTS

Cake pan
Parchment paper

Pencil
Scissors

METHOD

1. With a springform cake pan, put a sheet of parchment paper over the base, put the ring over it and close. Trim around the edges.

2. For fixed base pans, draw around the base onto parchment paper, cut this out, then put it on the greased base of the pan.

3. To line the sides of a round pan, cut parchment paper 1 in (2.5 cm) longer than the circumference and 3 in (7.5 cm) higher than the depth. Fold it down 1 in (2.5 cm) from the top, and cut incisions all the way along. With the incisions at the base, place this around the inside of the greased pan before adding the base lining. For a loaf pan, measure the width and length of the pan and add twice the depth. Cut parchment paper this size. Place the pan in the middle of the paper and make four cuts to the corners of the pan. Press into the greased pan overlapping the edges.

EXPERT TIPS

* Greasing the base of the pan before putting the paper in stops it moving around when you add the batter.

145 TESTING A CAKE FOR DONENESS

Learning this essential skill that will save you from turning out an overdone or underdone cake.

TOOLS AND INGREDIENTS

Skewer or knife
Cooked cake

METHOD

1 By touch, the cake should spring back when pressed with your fingertips if it is cooked through.

2 Alternatively, a skewer, knife or cake tester inserted into the center of the cake should come out clean with no traces of raw cake on it. If the cake isn't fully cooked, return it to the oven for a further 5 minutes, then check again.

EXPERT TIPS

* Ovens can vary, which means that cooking times will also vary. So keep a close eye on cakes as they get close to final cooking time. As you bake more cakes you will learn more about how your oven relates to cooking times for specific recipes and you will be able to judge whether to leave the cake in for a few minutes longer, or whether to take it out a few minutes earlier.

146 TURNING OUT AND COOLING A CAKE

If you have gone to the effort of baking a delicious homemade cake, it makes sense to learn the correct way to turn it out in order to retain its shape.

TOOLS AND INGREDIENTS

Table knife
Wire cooling rack

Dish towel
Cooked cake

METHOD

1. Carefully put the flat blade of a table knife inside the cake pan so that it lies flat against the edge. Run the knife around the edge of the cake in one smooth motion, keeping the flat of the knife against the pan at all times.

2. Put a wire cooling rack over the top of the cake pan.

3. Hold the cake pan with a dish towel and carefully flip it upside down out onto the wire rack. Give it a little shake to make sure the cake is fully loosened from the pan, then slowly pull the pan up and off the cake.

4. Gently peel off the parchment paper on the base of the cake and allow the cake to cool before turning the cake the right side up, onto a serving dish.

5. If you have used a springform pan, run a table knife around the edge of the cake, then release the ring from the base. Now slide the cake (on the parchment paper) from the pan base and onto a cooling rack. Once cool enough to handle, you can remove the parchment paper and allow to fully cool.

6. To remove a cake from a loose-bottomed pan, place a tin can or a jar on the work surface and put the cake pan on top gently easing the sides downward. Then transfer the cake to the cooling rack.

147 BEATING BUTTER AND SUGAR

This technique is used in such a large number of baking recipes that it makes sense to get it right from the start. There are certain tips that will help the cake batter achieve the correct consistency and this technique can be carried out by hand or by machine.

METHOD

1. By hand: put the required quantities of butter and sugar into a large mixing bowl. You can stand the bowl on a damp cloth to prevent it from slipping but this is not essential – some mixing bowls have rubber stoppers.

2. Beat the butter and sugar together with a wooden spoon until they are well combined and then continue until the mix is a pale yellow color and has a light and fluffy consistency.

3. If beating by machine, use the paddle attachment and beat the butter and sugar together until light and fluffy.

TOOLS AND INGREDIENTS

Large mixing bowl
Damp cloth (optional)
Wooden spoon
Electric mixer (if not beating by hand)

Butter (according to recipe)
Sugar (according to recipe`

EXPERT TIPS

* Make sure the butter is at room temperature. It helps if you cut it into small cubes before adding it to the bowl, as it will be easier to combine.

148 CUTTING IN

This technique, also known as rubbing in, is widely used in baking, particularly for pie crust, fruit crisps and some cookie recipes.

TOOLS AND INGREDIENTS

Large bowl
Damp cloth (optional)
Pastry blender (optional)

Butter (according to recipe)
Flour (according to recipe)

EXPERT TIPS

* Check through the bowl to make sure that all the "crumbs" are roughly the same size. Some recipes will call for coarse crumbs, others for fine but they should all be regular.

* Using a bigger mixing bowl will help to keep the ingredients moving around and give you space to fit both hands in easily to work with the mix.

METHOD

1. Put the required quantities of butter and flour into a large mixing bowl. You can stand the bowl on a damp cloth to prevent it from slipping but this is not essential.

2. Cut the butter and flour either by rubbing it between your fingers or by using a pastry blender until the mixture is the consistency of fine bread crumbs. Cutting in is the process of making the butter form into smaller and smaller chunks, but you don't want to melt it in the process.

3. As you cut in, lift your hands up so that you incorporate air into the batter and keep it light and cool.

149 BASIC YELLOW CAKE

By mastering the technique for a basic sponge cake, you are well on your way to baking greatness. This is one of the building blocks of bakery and it can be adapted to create an endless array of mouth-watering cakes.

TOOLS AND INGREDIENTS

Mixing bowl
Wooden spoon
Butter (according to recipe)

Sugar (according to recipe)
Eggs (according to recipe)
Flour (according to recipe)

EXPERT TIPS

* Once the batter is in the cake pan, give it a gentle shake to create an even layer and disperse any air bubbles.

* Make sure the oven is up to temperature before cooking the cake — it might sound obvious but baking requires precise working temperatures.

METHOD

1. Beat the butter and sugar together using the beating technique (see page 178).

2. Add the eggs, one at a time, beating well after each one so that each is fully incorporated before adding the next.

3. If the mix starts to curdle, add 1 tablespoon (15 ml) of flour from your weighed flour.

4. Add the remaining dry ingredients (according to recipe) and fold in (see page 193) until all the ingredients are fully incorporated.

5. Transfer the batter to a prepared cake pan (see pages 174–175) and cook in a preheated oven for the required time.

6. Test that it is done (see page 176) and turn out onto a wire rack (see page 177).

150 BASIC SPONGE CAKE

A whisked sponge differs from a yellow cake in that it doesn't contain any butter. Instead, eggs and sugar are beaten together over a pot of hot water.

TOOLS AND INGREDIENTS

Heatproof mixing bowl
Pot
Balloon whisk
Large rubber spatula
Eggs (according to recipe)
Sugar (according to recipe)
Flour (according to recipe)

EXPERT TIPS

* When a recipe says "holding a ribbon" it means that the batter will hold a ribbon shape for a few seconds when the whisk is lifted out of the bowl with some batter attached to it. The trail should then slowly disappear back into the remaining batter.

METHOD

1. Put the eggs and sugar in a large heatproof mixing bowl, placed over a pot of hot water. The bowl should be larger than the pot so that the base doesn't come into contact with the water.

2. Using a large balloon whisk, beat together the eggs and sugar until the batter is thick and creamy and will hold a ribbon (see expert tips, left) when lifted.

3. Remove the bowl from the heat and continue beating until the batter has cooled – this will take approximately 3–5 minutes.

4. Fold in the flour (see page 193) using a large rubber spatula, until it is just combined.

5. Transfer the batter to a prepared cake pan (see pages 174–175) and cook in a preheated oven for the required time.

151 ROLLING A ROULADE

A roulade is made from a thin sponge cake, which is topped with preserves and/or other fillings and carefully rolled to create a jelly roll. Your first roulade will probably be a daunting experience but if you follow these steps you can roll with confidence and you will soon become adept at the art, producing them all through the year and not just a Yule log for the holidays.

TOOLS AND INGREDIENTS

Parchment paper
Roulade sponge (according to recipe)
Confectioners' sugar

Filling (according to recipe)

METHOD

1. Put a large sheet of parchment paper onto a clean surface. Ensure the paper is larger than the roulade sponge so you have plenty of space to work around.

2. Dust the parchment paper liberally with confectioners' sugar.

3. Tip the cooled roulade sponge topside down, onto the dusted parchment paper. You need to do this quickly and with confidence; if you take too long the sponge is likely to tear or fall apart.

4. Spread the filling (according to recipe) evenly over the roulade. Leave a small margin around the outside of the roulade free of filling, as the filling will spread out when you roll up the roulade.

5. Starting at the short side closest to you, use the parchment paper to gently lift the roulade up and tip it forward to start rolling. Make sure the whole side is moving together so that the sponge doesn't break.

6. Slowly continue rolling, using the parchment paper as a guide, and roll the roulade entirely to the end. Finish with the end of the sponge on the underside of the roulade (or roll so that it falls there) to help keep the roulade intact.

⑥

EXPERT TIPS

* It is best to err on the side of caution when it comes to cooking the sponge. If it is even slightly overdone, it is more likely to crack and be less pliable when it comes to rolling.

* Don't worry if there is some cracking over the surface. This is normal and is fine as long as the sponge hasn't actually split.

* Allow the sponge to cool sufficiently before rolling so that it doesn't melt the filling.

152 GLAZE

This glossy, hard-setting frosting is used in many recipes, including cookies and cupcakes. The key to this technique is to achieve the right working consistency for the frosting – loose enough to work with but firm enough to stay on the top of the cakes.

TOOLS AND INGREDIENTS

Fine strainer
Large mixing bowl
Spoon
Whisk
Confectioners' sugar (according to recipe)
1 tbsp (15 ml) warm water
Flavoring of choice (or according to recipe)

EXPERT TIPS

* If you are adding decorations, do this while the frosting is still soft and runny.

* Add the water slowly – the frosting is easier to work with when it is fairly firm. If it is too runny, it won't create a thick layer on the cakes, but will simply run off.

METHOD

1. Sift the confectioners' sugar (according to recipe) into a large mixing bowl. Break any lumps with the back of a spoon so that the confectioners' sugar is fine and smooth.

2. Add 1 tablespoon (15 ml) of warm water and your flavoring of choice or according to recipe (vanilla, coffee etc.) and beat until the mixture is well combined. Add more water if necessary, a few drops at a time.

3. At this point, you should continue beating until the frosting is smooth. Add more liquid if necessary, until when you lift the spoon and let a ribbon of icing appear on the top of the mix, it takes exactly 10 seconds to melt back in. This is now the right consistency to work with.

153 BUTTERCREAM

As the name suggests, this cake topping is made with butter, giving it a rich, creamy texture and taste. It is used to ice cupcakes and simple cakes and is also used as a filling for layered cakes.

TOOLS AND INGREDIENTS

Wooden spoon
Large mixing bowl
Fine strainer
Softened butter (according to recipe)
Confectioners' sugar (according to recipe)
1-2 drops flavoring (personal preference
  or according to recipe)

EXPERT TIPS

* If you want to brighten up cakes, you can add a drop of food coloring to the frosting when you add the flavorings.

* For an even more creamy flavor, you can substitute warm milk for warm water, if you need to loosen the consistency.

METHOD

1. Beat the softened butter in a large mixing bowl with a wooden spoon until completely soft and smooth.

2. Gradually sift half of the confectioners' sugar over the butter, along with 1–2 drops of your chosen flavoring. Work slowly, beating until well combined before adding the remaining half of the confectioners' sugar.

3. Continue beating the frosting until the consistency is light and fluffy. If the frosting is stiff add a few drops of warm water and beat again. Repeat until you have the required consistency which will vary depending on how you are using your frosting. If you are spreading it on a cake, it wants to be soft but stiff enough to hold its shape. If you are piping it, you might want it a little bit firmer to give better definition.

154 FROSTING A CAKE

Baking a cake is a major culinary achievement but frosting it will take your skills up to another level. There are different techniques used for different types of frosting and the following steps should be followed when covering a cake with frosting such as buttercream (see page 185) or chocolate ganache (see page 33).

TOOLS AND INGREDIENTS

Cake decorating turntable, cake stand or serving plate
Spatula
Flat cake spatula knife or table knife

Cooked, cooled cake
Frosting of choice (e.g., buttercream or chocolate ganache)

METHOD

1. Put the cooked and cooled cake either on a turntable, a cake stand or serving plate.

2. Prepare the frosting according to the recipe.

3. Using a spatula, put half of the frosting on top of the cake, in the center.

4. Using a flat cake spatula, or a table knife, gradually spread the frosting out toward the edges of the cake in a smooth swirling motion. Check constantly to ensure that the frosting forms a uniform layer and that the whole cake is covered.

5. Rotate the turntable, stand or plate to reach all the edges without leaning over the cake, adding more frosting as needed.

6. Once the top of the cake is completely covered, either smooth it completely or make swirls from the center.

7. If frosting around the sides of the cake as well, use the cake spatula to spread the frosting evenly around the cake. Turn the turntable as you work and blend the frosting into the top layer to create a seamless coating.

EXPERT TIPS

* For an alternative finish, use a cake spatula to make soft peaks in the frosting on top of the cake (see above).

* For a thicker frosting finish, apply one layer of frosting then chill the cake for an hour in the refrigerator before applying another layer. This results in an even smoother finish so is ideal for special occasion cakes.

* Keep the frosting soft and pliable by adding a little warm water to it as you work, being careful to keep the consistency firm enough to coat the cake sufficiently.

155 USING A PASTRY BAG

If you feel ready to take your cake to a new level, then a few simple tools can help you achieve impressive results.

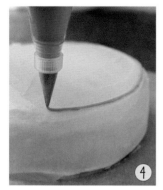 

TOOLS AND INGREDIENTS

Pastry bag and tips
Frosting
Cake, cupcakes or cookies

EXPERT TIPS

* It is very important to be high enough above the cake to be able to look down over it. Always keep pastry bag upright in your hand so that the frosting is falling directly onto the cake.

METHOD

1. Put your chosen tip (e.g., star) in the pastry bag then fold over the tip of the bag to form a lip that sits over your hand.

2. Fill the bag with your chosen frosting (e.g., buttercream, see page 185).

3. For a continuous pattern be sure to make sure there are no air bubbles in the bag: push all the frosting down in the bag so it is compact.

4. Hold the bag upright and apply light yet firm pressure as you move the bag around the cake edge. It is best to start on the opposite side of the cake and work around toward yourself.

5. For individual shapes (e.g., a rosette), hold the bag upright and pipe the shape onto the cake by squeezing and then pushing the pastry bag gently then pulling back up. Turn the cake as your work, don't lean over it.

156 FRUIT GLAZE

A fruit glaze is used to finish a cake, or it can be used as a base for frosting. While a lemon cake with a lemon glaze is a well-known, delicious staple, you could also glaze a chocolate cake with a cherry glaze, or a Bundt cake with apricot.

TOOLS AND INGREDIENTS

Pot
Fine strainer
Bowl
Pastry brush
Preserve or jelly (according to preference or recipe)

EXPERT TIPS

* As well as cakes, a fruit glaze can be used to top fruit tarts to add a bright sheen.

METHOD

1. Heat the preserve or jelly (according to preference or recipe) in a small pot over a medium heat until it is completely melted and has turned to liquid.

2. Pass the preserve through a fine strainer over a small bowl to remove any pieces of fruit (this step is unnecessary if using jelly).

3. If the glaze is too firm, add a splash of hot water and mix well.

4. To apply the glaze, dip a pastry brush in the liquid and brush all over the cooked and cooled cake. It is a good idea to put the cake on a turntable to apply the glaze, as you can move it around when glazing. Check the cake all over to ensure it is completely covered with a thin layer of glaze. The cake should have a glossy sheen.

157 MAKING FRENCH MERINGUE

Meringue is a simple but magical combination of egg whites and sugar. Meringue requires a long cooking time at a low temperature and the result is a crisp outside layer with a soft, chewy center.

TOOLS AND INGREDIENTS

Electric hand whisk
Mixing bowl
Baking sheet
Parchment paper

3 egg whites
¾ cup (150 g) superfine
  sugar

EXPERT TIPS

* The ratio of sugar to eggs is ¼ cup (2 oz or 50 g) per egg white, so you can adjust the recipe to make more or less meringue accordingly.

* Oven temperature is key to successful meringues. If yours are coming out too crunchy, try turning the oven down to its lowest setting.

METHOD

1. Separate the eggs (see page 159). Set aside the yolks to use in another recipe.

2. Using an electric hand whisk, beat the egg whites in a bowl until they form stiff peaks (see page 165). You should start with a fairly low speed and gradually build this up.

3. Gradually add the sugar. This should be added to the egg whites 1 tablespoon at a time, beating until it is completely incorporated and then adding the next tablespoon. Continue adding the sugar and beating until the meringue mixture is stiff and shiny.

4. Line a baking sheet with parchment paper. Spoon the mixture into meringues the size and shape you require. Put the meringues in a preheated oven at 275°F (140°C) and bake for 1 hour (or according to individual recipe). Once cooked, switch off the oven but leave the meringues in the oven, with the door slightly ajar, until it has cooled.

158 MAKING ITALIAN MERINGUE

Italian meringue is a firm meringue that is ready to use as soon as the mixture is combined and cooled – there is no need to cook it.

TOOLS AND INGREDIENTS

Small pot
Food mixer
Cup
Teaspoon
1 cup and 2 tbsp (250 g) superfine
    sugar
4 tbsp (60 ml) water
4 egg whites

METHOD

1 Start with a sugar syrup (see page 32) or combine 1 cup and 2 tablespoons (250 g) sugar and 4 tablespoons (60 ml) water in a small pot. Bring the sugar mixture to a boil and, once the syrup is at the soft-ball stage, remove the pot from heat. The soft-ball stage means that when you drop a teaspoonful of the mixture into a cup or small bowl of cold water to cool it down, it will form a soft ball.

2 Whisk 4 egg whites in a free-standing mixer until they are stiff and hold a peak.

3 At this point, pour the sugar syrup in a steady stream into the egg whites. Continue until the egg whites are stiff and glossy. Keep beating the meringue mix until is has cooled, then it is ready to use.

159 PAVLOVA

A pavlova is the ultimate meringue-based dessert. Once the basic meringue mix is made, this is what can be achieved. The actual fillings and toppings come down to personal preference but the meringue itself should be crisp and crunchy on the outside, with a softer center.

TOOLS AND INGREDIENTS

Electric hand whisk
Mixing bowl
Baking sheet
Parchment paper
Cake spatula or serving
  spoon

3 egg whites
¾ cup (150 g) superfine
  sugar
Filling and toppings
  (according to recipe or
  personal choice)

EXPERT TIPS

* A classic pavlova filling is firmly whipped heavy cream spread in the center of the meringue and topped with fresh fruit, such as summer berries, or sliced exotic fruit.

* To keep the parchment paper flat against the baking sheet, use tiny dots of the meringue mixture to stick the paper down at each corner.

METHOD

1. Prepare the meringue mixture (see page 190).

2. Cover a large baking sheet with parchment paper and spread the meringue into a circular shape in the center of the paper. Use a cake spatula or a serving spoon to shape the meringue so that it dips in the center and builds up around the edges.

3. The final shape should look similar to a bird's nest.

4. Place the baking tray in a preheated oven at 350°F (180°C) for 5 minutes, then lower the temperature to 250°F (120°C) and bake for 1 hour (or according to individual recipe). Once cooked, switch off the oven but leave the meringue in the oven until it has cooled.

5. Remove the cooled meringue from the parchment paper and put on a serving dish.

6. If filling with cream, whip the required amount of heavy cream until it forms stiff peaks. Top the cream with your choice of toppings.

160 FOLDING IN EGG WHITES

The idea behind folding in egg whites is to try and retain as much air in the whites as possible. You have to combine the ingredients with as little interference as possible – every mix with the spoon releases more air, so the fewer folds it takes, the better.

TOOLS AND INGREDIENTS

Balloon whisk
Large bowl
Large metal spoon

Beaten egg whites (see page 165)

METHOD

1 Once the egg whites are beaten to the correct consistency (see page 165), gently fold them into the required mixture using a large metal spoon.

2 Fold the egg whites in by gently cutting the mixture in half and folding over to gradually incorporate the whites. Repeat and rotate the bowl as you fold, to ensure the whole mixture is exposed to the egg whites and that they are uniformly mixed.

3 Make sure you don't over-mix the ingredients and knock the air out of the mixture. This means taking time and working with a light touch. Always carefully cut through the mixture with the spoon, and never push it down flat into the bowl.

161 FOLDING IN FLOUR

The key to a light-as-a-feather sponge cake is to incorporate as much air as possible into the batter. Beating the ingredients together starts the process, and folding in sifted flour (see page 196) completes it.

TOOLS AND INGREDIENTS

Large bowl
Strainer

Large metal spoon or plastic spatula
Flour

METHOD

1 Sift the flour onto the other cake ingredients as required by the recipe.

2 Using the metal spoon, gently cut through the flour and cake mixture and turn it over so the ingredients are combined.

162 PHYLLO PASTRY

This light and incredibly thin pastry is used for cakes and desserts and must be handled carefully. Buy it ready made from stores, rather than trying to make it yourself!

TOOLS AND INGREDIENTS

Damp cloth or dish towel
Baking sheet
Pastry brush
Phyllo pastry
Melted butter

EXPERT TIPS

* Layering the sheets of pastry with butter gives them strength and also helps them to rise, which results in the distinctive puffed, crispy finish once the pastry has been baked.

METHOD

1. Gently melt a knob of butter in a small pan and transfer to a bowl or small dish.

2. Unwrap the phyllo pastry and keep it covered with a damp cloth or dish towel when not using because it can quickly dry out due to its paper-thin layers.

3. Carefully peel off the first sheet of dough and lay it flat on a greased baking sheet. Use a pastry brush to brush the first layer of dough all over with a thin, even layer of melted butter.

4. Lay the next sheet of dough on top of the first and brush it all over with butter. Repeat with the remaining sheets of dough.

163 WHIPPING CREAM

If you need whipped cream for a recipe or to serve alongside a dessert, brace yourself for a workout. It takes time so don't give up – eventually all the hard work will pay off and the cream will thicken.

TOOLS AND INGREDIENTS

Large mixing bowl
Damp cloth (optional)
Large balloon whisk

Heavy cream (according to recipe)

METHOD

1. Put the cream in a large mixing bowl. If preferred, you can place the bowl on a damp cloth to prevent it from slipping.

2. Using a large balloon whisk, beat the cream in a large circular motion, from the base of the bowl upward.

3. Continue until the required stiffness is achieved.

EXPERT TIPS

* If you use an electric whisk, be careful toward the end as your cream can quickly turn to too thick.

164 BAIN-MARIE (FOR CHOCOLATE)

This is a gentle way to melt chocolate, ensuring it melts slowly and evenly, as a consistent heat is applied below it.

TOOLS AND INGREDIENTS

Heatproof bowl
Pot
Chocolate (according to recipe)

METHOD

1. Break the chocolate into pieces and put in a heatproof bowl.

2. Select a pot in which the bowl sits in snugly, without the base touching the bottom of the bowl (should be a gap of several inches).

3. Put enough cold water in the pot to stop the pot boiling dry, but not so much that it touches the base of the bowl. Set the pot (with the heatproof bowl over it) over a medium heat.

4. When the water comes to a boil, reduce the heat and then turn off once the chocolate is melted.

165 FLAMBÉING

This skill involves burning alcohol that has been added to ingredients in a skillet. It is a dramatic culinary effect but also adds flavor.

TOOLS AND INGREDIENTS

Medium skillet
Long-handled metal spoon
Knob of butter
Sugar (according to recipe)

Fruit (according to recipe)
Liquor or spirit (according to recipe)

METHOD

1. Turn off extractor fan if using. Melt a knob of butter in a medium skillet. Add the sugar and fruit, and gently cook for about 2 minutes, shaking the skillet so that all the fruit is coated in the melted sugar.

2. Heat the alcohol in a separate pot until hot. Carefully light the alcohol and when it is flaming, pour it over the fruit.

3. Using a long-handled spoon, baste the fruit with flaming alcohol until the flame dies down.

EXPERT TIPS

* To light the fruit, tilt the skillet towards the flame until it catches alight, or use a match.

166 SIFTING (FLOUR, CONFECTIONERS' SUGAR, COCOA)

This skill is essential for any baker.

TOOLS AND INGREDIENTS

Fine strainer
Large mixing bowl
Spoon

Ingredients (e.g., flour, confectioners' sugar, cocoa powder)

METHOD

1. Put the fine strainer over a large mixing bowl and pour in the dry ingredient.

2. Gently shake the fine strainer to transfer the ingredients into the bowl, breaking any lumps with the back of a spoon.

167 DISSOLVING GELATIN

Gelatin is used for set desserts such as mousses, fruit gelatins and in gelatin salads. It comes in powdered and leaf form.

EXPERT TIPS

* Don't allow gelatin water to boil, as it becomes stringy.

* Don't stir the gelatin when preparing.

* Powdered gelatin is suitable for vegetarians but leaf gelatin has meat extract in it so bear this in mind if you have vegetarians coming for dinner.

* Both types of gelatin are interchangeable when using them in recipes; it comes down to personal preference.

TOOLS AND INGREDIENTS

Bowl   Pot
Gelatin

METHOD (POWDER GELATIN)

1. Sprinkle the powdered gelatin over 5 tablespoons (75 ml) cold water in a medium heatproof bowl.

2. Allow to stand for 5 minutes until the gelatin is spongy.

3. Put the bowl over a pot of hot water until the liquid turns clear and is ready to use in the recipe.

METHOD (LEAF GELATIN)

1. Soak the gelatin leaves in cold water for about 5 minutes until they are completely softened. Squeeze out the excess water from the gelatin leaves.

2. Transfer the leaves to a bowl of hot water and leave to dissolve.

PASTA, GRAIN, LEGUME AND BREAD SKILLS

Pastas, breads, grains, legumes and rice form the staple diet for the majority of people in the world. High in carbohydrates, these foods are filling and nutritious. However, that doesn't mean that they are all straightforward to prepare and cook – each requires you to master specific techniques in order to get the very best from the ingredient.

This chapter will take you through the essential skills for cooking with these everyday ingredients that make up the mainstay of our daily menus. You will learn how to prepare fresh pasta (as well as how to roll it and cook it), how to make a basic risotto and how to prepare dried beans, grains and legumes. With the right equipment and knowledge, heavy and uninspiring rice can forever be avoided and overcooked pasta will be a dim and distant memory.

168 MAKING FRESH PASTA

If you have looked on in wonder as chefs prepare fresh pasta in restaurants or on television programs, this skill will dispel the myth. Fresh pasta is actually surprisingly easy to make; it just takes a little time and patience and a gentle touch to create the silky smooth pasta dough.

TOOLS AND INGREDIENTS

Fork (optional)
Pastry scraper
Large mixing bowl
Plastic wrap
3¼ cups (400 g) "00"
   flour (see expert tip)

4 eggs, beaten
1 tbsp (15 ml) olive oil
Salt

METHOD

1. Pour the flour onto a clean surface and make a well in the center using your fingers. Pour the beaten eggs into the well, with the olive oil and salt.

2. Mix the ingredients together with your hands, or using a fork, until the mixture is well combined. You can use a pastry scraper to incorporate everything into a central ball of mixture. This should be moist but not too sticky. If it is, sprinkle over a little more flour.

3. Knead the dough for approximately 15 minutes by stretching and pushing it away from you, using the heel of your hand. When finished, the dough should be smooth and have an elastic quality. If the dough becomes too dry, add a little more olive oil; if it is too wet, sprinkle over more flour.

4. Once the dough is finished, put in a large mixing bowl, cover with plastic wrap and rest for 1 hour.

EXPERT TIPS

* "00" flour is a very fine Italian flour that is used primarily for fresh pasta recipes and some cakes and cookies.

* You can mix the ingredients together in a food processor to save time but keep a close eye on the dough so that it is not over-worked.

* Don't add all the eggs at once – add most of them and start combining the dough. If it is looking sticky at this point you don't need to add the last of the eggs.

169 ROLLING FRESH PASTA

The work isn't over when the dough is made – proper rolling can make all the difference to the taste of the finished pasta.

TOOLS AND INGREDIENTS

Large chef's knife   Prepared pasta dough
Pasta machine

METHOD

1. Cut the prepared and rested pasta dough into 4 equal pieces and flatten them into rough rectangular shapes.

2. Put the first piece into the pasta machine, on the widest setting, and roll it through slowly and constantly, supporting the pasta as it passes out of the machine.

3. Fold the piece into thirds and roll through the pasta machine again. Repeat another 3 or 4 times, but without folding the piece of pasta again. Each time you roll, reduce the width setting of the pasta machine.

170 CUTTING FRESH PASTA

Make light work of cutting pasta dough by using the settings on the pasta machine.

TOOLS AND INGREDIENTS

Pasta machine   Prepared pasta dough
Drying rack

METHOD

1. Set the machine to cut the pasta into strips.

2. Hang the pasta to dry (see expert tips) and repeat with the remaining 3 pieces.

EXPERT TIPS

* If you are making a lot of pasta, a clothes rack is ideal for hanging the pasta. It needs plenty of space so the strands don't stick together while it is still moist. Make sure the clothes rack is clean before using it.

171 COOKING PASTA

It might sound simple but there is a knack to correctly boiling pasta, in order to keep the texture but ensure it is cooked through.

TOOLS AND INGREDIENTS

Large pot
Wooden spoon

Strainer
1 tbsp (15 ml) salt
Pasta

METHOD

1. Bring a large pot of water to a rolling boil.

2. Add 1 tbsp (15 ml) salt to the water and allow it to return to a boil.

3. Pour the pasta into the water and gently stir to make sure that the strands or pieces are all separate and don't stick together in a large lump in the pot.

EXPERT TIPS

* Perfectly cooked pasta should be al dente (retain a little bite) so keep a close eye on the cooking time and keep checking the pasta. Fresh pasta only requires a few minutes of cooking time, unlike dry pasta, so this is very important.

* Use a very large pot so that the pasta has plenty of space to move around as it cooks and expands.

* Once the pasta has drained, mix it with the sauce immediately, otherwise it will stick together and will then be difficult to separate.

* Always serve the sauce mixed through the pasta – not spooned into the center. Again, this stops the pasta from sticking.

4. Cook for the required time, stirring occasionally.

5. Drain the pasta into a strainer.

172 RAVIOLI

These delicate pasta parcels taste so much nicer if you have made them yourself. Ravioli will bring together a number of skills so this is a good technique to aim for, once you have mastered the art of making and rolling out fresh pasta.

(4)

TOOLS AND INGREDIENTS

Rolling pin
Cutting board
Pastry wheel or sharp
  chef's knife
Pastry brush

Pasta dough (see pages
  200–201)
Flour, for dusting
Ravioli filling (according
  to recipe)
Egg yolk
Slotted spoon

METHOD

1. Make a batch of fresh pasta dough (see pages 200–201).

2. Knead the pasta and roll it out into a large sheet (see page 202).

3. Put the pasta sheet on a lightly floured surface and trim the edges so that it is an even rectangular shape.

4. Put small mounds of the ravioli filling (according to recipe) evenly across one half of the sheet, leaving sufficient space around each mound of filling to seal and cut around.

5. Using a pastry brush, brush around the outside of each mound with a beaten egg yolk.

6. Gently pull and fold the other half of the pasta sheet over the filling and gently press

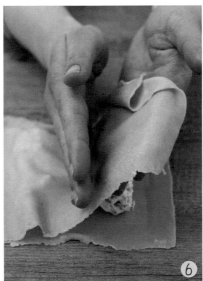

down around each mound of filling with your fingertips. Make sure there are no air bubbles and that the ravioli parcels are tightly sealed.

7. Now cut around each mound, leaving a border of pasta dough. You can use either a pasta wheel or sharp chef's knife to do this.

8. Most ravioli will take about 4–5 minutes to cook, in a large pot of boiling water. Remove with a slotted spoon and serve with a sauce or just a drizzle of butter or olive oil.

EXPERT TIPS

* If you plan to make a lot of your own ravioli, you might want to buy a ravioli press or rolling pin to ensure perfect shapes every time.

* Make sure all the water has drained from the ravioli before you put them on a serving plate.

* If you are making a lot of pasta, keep the prepared ravioli on a clean dish towel and cover with another – this will stop the pasta from drying out.

173 SOAKING RICE NOODLES

Rice noodles can be used in a wide variety of dishes from stir-fries to soups. It is important to soak them fully before using in a recipe, as they need to be completely softened.

TOOLS AND INGREDIENTS

Large heatproof bowl
Fork
Large strainer
Noodles

METHOD

1. If the noodles are in stacks in the package, gently ease them apart and put the required amount into a large heatproof bowl.

2. Pour over enough boiling water so that the noodles are completely submerged.

3. Let the noodles stand for 2 minutes then break apart gently with a fork so that they are all separate strands.

4. Leave the noodles in the water for about another 5 minutes, or until they are completely softened.

5. Drain the noodles into a large strainer and rinse well in cold water.

EXPERT TIPS

* Use the noodles immediately so they don't stick together.

* If you need to wait for a few minutes before adding the noodles to the recipe, you can pour a small amount of oil over the drained noodles to keep them from sticking together.

174 SOAKING AND COOKING DRIED BEANS

Dried beans need a lot of soaking before they are sufficiently rehydrated to use in recipes. Although it is time consuming, there is little effort involved and it makes economical sense to use dried beans, rather than canned beans, in recipes.

TOOLS AND INGREDIENTS

Large bowl   Large pot
Large strainer
Beans

EXPERT TIPS

* If you can let the beans soak overnight, all the better.

* To tell if the beans are cooked through, try squashing one – it should yield easily. If not quite cooked, return to the heat for another 20 minutes then check again.

METHOD

1. Sort through the beans and discard any that are discolored or misshapen. Put the beans in a large strainer and rinse under cold running water to remove any grit.

2. Put the beans in a large bowl and cover with enough cold water to completely submerge them.

3. Cover and let soak for a minimum of 8 hours (or overnight).

4. Drain the beans in a large strainer and rinse thoroughly under cold, running water.

5. Transfer the beans to a large pot and cover with enough fresh, cold water so they are completely submerged.

6. Bring the water to a boil and simmer the beans for the required cooking time.

7. Drain well and use.

175 COOKING RICE: HOT WATER METHOD

Many people fail miserably when it comes to cooking perfect fluffy rice – it either ends up heavy or undercooked. However, if you follow this simple technique, your rice should be perfectly cooked every time.

TOOLS AND INGREDIENTS

Large pot
Wooden spoon
Fine strainer
Rice
Pinch of salt

EXPERT TIPS

* Always add plenty of water to the pot as rice expands a lot during cooking.

* Make sure the water is boiling before adding the rice to the pot.

METHOD

1. Wash the rice thoroughly in cold water first.

2. Bring a large pot of water to a boil and add a pinch of salt.

3. Add the rice to the pot and stir with a wooden spoon in order to separate the grains in the water.

4. Gently simmer the rice for the required cooking time (different varieties of rice require slightly different cooking times so always check the packaging to get the correct time).

5. Drain the rice in a fine strainer and rinse with boiling water to remove any impurities and rinse off some of the starch. This will help to keep the rice fluffy and stop the grains sticking together.

176 COOKING RICE: ABSORPTION METHOD

For this cooking method you use 2½ parts water to 1 part rice. You need to be confident and avoid checking the rice during cooking, as this will release the steam and slow down the cooking process.

TOOLS AND INGREDIENTS

Large pot with lid
Fork
Rice
Pinch of salt

EXPERT TIPS

* This method only works if the rice is perfectly cooked but obviously this is difficult to check. If you are unsure, try a few grains and leave for a few minutes longer if there is still bite to the rice.

* If you use a pot with a clear lid, it will be easier to see if there is still a lot of liquid in the pot and the rice therefore needs to cook for longer.

METHOD

1. Put the water and rice (2½ times the volume of water to rice) and a generous pinch of salt in a large pot over a medium heat and cover.

2. Simmer the rice for 15 minutes (for white rice; 35–40 minutes for brown rice) and then remove from the heat.

3. Let stand for 5 minutes and then fluff the rice with a fork to separate the grains.

177 COOKING STICKY RICE AND SUSHI RICE

While boiled or steamed rice should be light and fluffy with separate grains, sticky rice and sushi rice need to be heavy, with full grains that stick to each other for their respective recipes' uses.

METHOD

1. Put the rice in a large fine strainer and rinse under cold, running water. Continue until the water runs clear.

2. Soak the rice in fresh cold water in a large bowl for 30 minutes then drain well.

3. Put the rinsed and soaked rice in a large pot, covering with plenty of cold water.

4. Bring the water to a boil, cover with a lid and reduce the heat. Simmer for 15 minutes.

5. Remove from the heat, leave the rice covered in the pot and let stand for 15 minutes before serving.

EXPERT TIPS

* Soaking the rice in water before cooking helps it to absorb moisture and become more glutinous during the cooking process.

* If you have more time, you can let the rice soak for up to 4 hours before cooking it.

TOOLS AND INGREDIENTS

Large, fine strainer
Large bowl
Large pot with lid
Rice

178 COOKING JAPANESE RICE

Although cooked in a similar way to sticky rice, this method adds extra ingredients at the end of cooking in order to make the rice ready to be used for sushi.

TOOLS AND INGREDIENTS

Large, fine strainer
Large bowl
Large pot with lid
Small pot
Mixing bowl
Wooden spoon

1 cup (180 g) rice
4 tbsp (60 ml) rice
  vinegar
4 tbsp (60 ml) superfine
  sugar
Pinch of salt

EXPERT TIPS

* Cooling the rice helps to remove any excess moisture so that the rice is not too damp when it is used for sushi.

METHOD

1. Put the rice in a large fine strainer and rinse under cold running water. Continue until the water runs clear.

2. Cook the rice (according to package instructions) and let cool, covered, for 15 minutes.

3. In a small pot mix 4 tbsp (60 ml) rice vinegar, 4 tbsp (60 ml) sugar and a pinch of salt. Bring to a boil and simmer until the sugar has completely dissolved then remove from the heat and let cool.

4. Put the cooled rice in a large mixing bowl and pour over the vinegar syrup.

5. Mix the two together using a wooden spoon and fluff the rice up while mixing.

6. Either use immediately or cover the rice with a damp dish towel until needed.

179 BASIC RISOTTO

There is nothing more comforting than the thick, creamy consistency of a risotto. This labor-intensive meal is well worth the effort and the constant stirring is actually a very relaxing way to watch a dish being created.

TOOLS AND INGREDIENTS

Small pot
Large pot
Wooden spoon
Knob of butter
1 tbsp (15 ml) olive oil
1 onion, finely chopped
4 cups (1 L) vegetable
  broth
2 cups (400 g) risotto
  (e.g., arborio) rice
4 fl oz (125 ml) white
  wine
3½ fl oz (100 ml) Pernod
½ cup (50 g) shredded
  Parmesan cheese

METHOD

1. Put the broth in a small pot and keep this over a low heat.

2. In a large pot, heat the butter and olive oil and gently sauté the onion over a low heat until softened, approximately 10 minutes.

3. Add the risotto rice and stir until all the grains are well coated.

4. Increase the heat and pour over the white wine and Pernod and simmer until the alcohol has been absorbed into the rice.

5. Add a ladleful of hot broth to the large pot and stir continuously until most of the liquid has been absorbed by the rice. Add the next ladleful and continue, gradually adding all the broth to the rice.

6. The risotto will start to swell and look glossy.

7. The risotto is cooked when the rice is al dente (still has a slight bite to each grain) and will take about 20 minutes. The amount of broth needed can vary and you might use a little more or less for the risotto.

8. Once the rice is almost cooked through, stir in half the Parmesan, remove the large pot from the heat and cover. Rest for 2–3 minutes so that the rice very gradually absorbs the remaining liquid.

9. Stir through the remaining Parmesan and serve.

EXPERT TIPS

* You can add any number of ingredients to this basic recipe. Stir in cooked tiger shrimp and a handful of small green peas a couple of minutes before the end of the cooking; add some chopped chorizo, mushrooms or prosciutto; or add steamed asparagus spears just before serving.

* Always use risotto (such as arborio) rice for the recipe – other varieties won't soak up enough liquid to swell and become glutinous.

180 COOKING POLENTA

This northern Italian staple made from fine ground corn can be served as a creamy accompaniment to meat sauces, stews or other meat or fish dishes. It can also be cooled and served in slices.

TOOLS AND INGREDIENTS

Pot
Whisk
Polenta
Pinch of salt

Knob of butter
Milk
Handful of shredded
  Parmesan cheese

EXPERT TIPS

* Quick-cook polenta makes a speedy accompaniment – serve as you would mashed potatoes, with a little butter melted and plenty of seasoning.

METHOD (WET)

1. Bring the required amount of water to a boil and add salt (different types of polenta require different amounts of liquid and different cooking times, so always check the package instructions before cooking).

2. While continuously whisking the water, pour in the required amount of polenta, then reduce the heat.

3. Add the butter and a little milk and beat for several minutes until the polenta is cooked.

4. If the consistency is still very thick, you can add more milk. Finish by stirring through a handful of shredded Parmesan, if you like.

METHOD (HARD)

1. Spread the cooked polenta (see above) on an oiled baking sheet, leave to cool and set.

2. Cut the polenta block into the required sizes to use. Grill the cut blocks of polenta before serving, if desired.

181 COOKING QUINOA, FARRO AND BARLEY

Nutritious, delicious and easy to prepare, quinoa, farro and barley can be substituted for rice or couscous when you're looking for a hearty accompaniment to a meal, or some bulk for stews and casseroles. All of these grains are very easy to cook.

TOOLS AND INGREDIENTS

Large strainer
Large pot
Grains

EXPERT TIPS

* Cook these grains like rice so that they still retain a slight bite (al dente).

* Barley is wonderful for soups and stews and can also be substituted for rice. As a whole grain it is a nutritious addition to your diet.

METHOD

1. Rinse the grains well in a large strainer under cold running water then put in a large pot and cover completely with cold water.

2. Bring to a boil and cook for the required time (the cooking time for each ingredient varies so always check the packaging before cooking and keep a close eye on timings).

3. Drain the grains well and use as required.

182 COOKING COUSCOUS

There are different methods for cooking couscous but the one below will ensure the grains remain fluffy and light. The couscous should soak up all the liquid but be careful – too much liquid will result in a sticky, sloppy mess.

TOOLS AND INGREDIENTS

Large heatproof bowl
Fork
Couscous

Salt and black pepper
Olive oil

METHOD

1. Pour the required quantity of couscous into a large heatproof bowl.

2. Sprinkle over salt and pepper and drizzle with a little olive oil.

3. Pour over enough boiling water to come just above the top of the couscous.

4. Cover the bowl and let the couscous stand and soak up the water for 5–10 minutes.

5. Gently fluff up the couscous with a fork, separating the grains.

EXPERT TIPS

* You can leave the couscous for longer if you need to, it will still fluff up with a fork. However, don't leave it for too long or it will start to harden.

* Serve with roasted vegetables and crumbled feta cheese for a lunch dish or barbecue accompaniment. It also works well with chopped mint, chopped chilies, garbanzo beans and a dash of lemon juice, or as a filling for roasted zucchinis or peppers.

183 COOKING BULGUR WHEAT

This is cooked in much the same way as couscous (see opposite), with the grains soaking up sufficient water to become enlarged and fluffy but without becoming waterlogged and soggy.

METHOD

1. Rinse the required amount of bulgur wheat in a fine large strainer under cold running water then put in a large heatproof bowl.

2. Sprinkle over a little salt and pepper and drizzle with olive oil.

3. Pour over enough boiling water so that the bulgur wheat is covered and there is a very thin later of water on the surface.

4. Cover the bowl and let stand for 15–20 minutes to enable the grains to soak up all the liquid.

5. Fluff up the bulgur wheat with a fork and serve hot or cold.

TOOLS AND INGREDIENTS

Large strainer   Olive oil
Large heatproof bowl
Fork
Bulgur wheat
Salt and black pepper

EXPERT TIPS

* Use in the same way as rice or couscous – either as the main carbohydrate in a meal drizzled with a little olive oil or lemon juice, or as the basis for a salad or stuffing.

* The addition of olive oil helps to stop the grains from sticking together while they soak up the water.

184 COOKING LENTILS

There are a number of different varieties of lentils but they all share a rich, earthy flavor and are packed full of essential minerals and vitamins.

TOOLS AND INGREDIENTS

Strainer
Large pot with lid
Lentils (according to recipe)

EXPERT TIPS

* If you soak the lentils in cold water for an hour before cooking, this will reduce the cooking time dramatically.

* Red and yellow lentils cook the quickest (about 15–20 minutes) while green lentils take the longest (about 40 minutes) so always check the instructions on the packaging before cooking.

METHOD

1. Put the lentils (variety according to recipe or preference) in a large strainer and rinse under cold running water. Transfer to a large pot and cover with plenty of cold water. Do not add salt, as this will toughen the lentils.

2. Cover the pot with a lid and bring to a boil.

3. Remove the lid and continue to boil the lentils for the required cooking time (according to package instructions), adding more water if needed (they soak up a lot of water so it may need topping up).

4. Drain well and use.

185 MAKING BREAD CRUMBS

From toppings for pasta and vegetable dishes, to bulk for stuffings and sauces, bread crumbs are an indispensable kitchen staple. But don't buy them – make your own fresh bread crumbs. It's easier than you might think.

METHOD

1. Tear slices of fresh torn-up bread, with the crusts removed, into a food processor (it's fine if the bread is a day or two old).

2. Pulse gently until you have fine crumbs.

3. For extra fine bread crumbs, sieve the crumbs through a fine strainer over a bowl.

EXPERT TIPS

* For rough crumbs, you can simply rub torn-up pieces of bread between your fingers — crusts included. You will end up with a mixed selection of sizes, which can be combined with shredded cheese for a crunchy pasta topping. For additional flavor you can add freshly chopped herbs, or a sprinkling of spice.

* Make the bread crumbs in large batches and keep them in the freezer. This is a great way to use up odds and ends of bread, or the last slice in the bag that nobody wants to eat.

TOOLS AND INGREDIENTS

Food processor
Fine strainer (optional)
Bread

186 CROUTONS

Crunchy croutons add an extra dimension to a bowl of soup or a fresh salad, especially when they are homemade.

TOOLS AND INGREDIENTS

Sharp chef's knife
Cutting board
Skillet

Paper towel
Olive oil
Bread (thick, white slices)

EXPERT TIPS

* Don't scrimp on the bread – unlike bread crumbs, you will taste the flavor of the crouton so use a good quality bread.

* Denser breads such as sourdough work especially well as they will hold their shape in the skillet.

* If you want your croutons to have a more rustic look, you can tear the bread into small pieces rather than cutting it.

METHOD

1 Cut thick slices of white bread into even cubes of desired size (you can choose large croutons for soups, or smaller croutons for sprinkling over salads – as long as they are all the same size so they cook evenly).

2 Heat the olive oil in a skillet (enough so there is a very thin layer covering the base of the skillet).

3. Once the oil is hot, add the bread cubes and toss in the skillet so they are all well coated in the oil.

4. Continue to move around the skillet for a further 2–3 minutes until the cubes are a golden color all over.

5. Drain on a paper towel to remove the excess olive oil.

187 CROUTES

A croute is like a giant crouton or – in another way of thinking – it is like a very crisp piece of toast. These can be presented like crostini.

TOOLS AND INGREDIENTS

Sliced bread
Cutting board
Chef's knife

EXPERT TIPS

Bruschetta

* Thick slices of bread toasted with topping such as tomato, onion, garlic and olive oil.

METHOD

1. Heat the broiler until hot.

2. Slice your chosen bread into medium slices. Make sure all the pieces are the same size.

3. Arrange the bread slices on a broiler pan or rack and put under the broiler.

4. Turn the slices after 2 minutes and toast for a further 2 minutes, then remove from the broiler. Timings will vary for different ovens and different varieties of bread, so keep a close eye while they are toasting. The croutes should be golden and crispy but not overdone.

EXPERT TIPS

* Try a simple topping of tomato, basil and mozzarella, or crushed pea and mint – these make great appetizers or canapés.

188 MELBA TOAST

These can be served cold to accompany pâté or mousse.

TOOLS AND INGREDIENTS

Serrated knife
Baking sheet
White bread

EXPERT TIPS

* These delicate toast slices are ideal for serving with pâté or savory mousse.

* If you want more uniform shapes and don't want the sides to curl up, flatten the toasts between two baking sheets for a minute when they come out of the oven. This should help them to stay flat.

METHOD

1. Lightly toast slices of white bread (in the toaster or under a preheated, hot broiler) and cool.

2. Preheat the oven to 350°F (180°C).

3. Slice each piece of toast in half horizontally – a serrated knife is best for this. The cut them in half diagonally to make triangles.

4. Put the thin slices of toast on a baking sheet with the untoasted side facing up.

5. Bake the slices for approximately 5–10 minutes. They should have a golden color and the ends should curl up.

189 GARLIC CROUTES

If you've ever eaten in a tapas restaurant, chances are you have eaten bread this way. You will be amazed at the amount of flavor that can be packed into the bread by simply rubbing it with a garlic clove.

TOOLS AND INGREDIENTS

Bread knife
Pastry brush (optional)
Bread

Garlic clove
Olive oil

EXPERT TIPS

* For even more flavor, cut a large tomato in half and rub the cut side over the toast after the garlic.

* You can use virtually any variety of bread for this technique, although breads such as ciabatta and French bread are easy to cut and toast, and easy to handle once cooked.

METHOD

1. Cut thin slices of bread from a fresh loaf, ensuring they are all the same thickness.

2. Toast the bread in a toaster or under a preheated, hot broiler.

3. Cut a garlic clove in half lengthwise.

4. When the bread is crisp and toasted through, remove from the broiler pan and rub with the cut side of the garlic clove all over the toast. Alternatively, you can use a pastry brush to brush the toast slices with olive oil.

BROTH SKILLS

It might be easy to crumble a bouillon cube into a bowl of hot water but it has nowhere near the intense depth of flavor that a home-cooked broth does. If you regularly cook roast dinners, prepare whole poultry or game birds, or large joints of meat, it makes sense to prepare you own broth. Not only are you being more economical by using every last scrap of the meat and vegetables, but you will also benefit from the rich, intense flavor that comes from the lengthy boiling of carcasses and bones.

In this chapter you will learn how to create all the basic broths from scratch. As with many skills, these are easy to master, requiring nothing more than an investment of time and a little forward thinking.

190 CHICKEN OR GAME BROTH

If you thought freshly prepared broths were the preserve of professional chefs and practiced home cooks, think again. Anyone can make a delicious chicken broth from scratch and once you have tasted your homemade version, you'll never reach for the bouillon cubes again.

TOOLS AND INGREDIENTS

Large pot
Sharp chef's knife
Cutting board
Skimming spoon or large
  flat spoon
Fine strainer
Large bowl

Chicken carcass, plus
  leftover meat
5 oz (150 g) chopped
  onion, celery and carrot
5 whole black peppercorns
1 bouquet garni (see page
  62)

METHOD

1. Put the chicken carcass, or any bones and leftover meat, into a large pot. Make sure you have picked off the majority of meat before making the broth – it's amazing how much meat can be left behind.

2. Add approximately 5 ounces (150 grams) mixture of rough chopped onion, celery and carrot, with 5 whole black peppercorns and 1 bouquet garni (see page 62).

3. Add 6½ cups (1½ liters) of cold water to the pot.

4. Bring to a boil and simmer for 2-3 hours. Using a skimming spoon, or large flat spoon, skim the surface of the broth frequently to remove the scum.

5. Strain the broth through a fine strainer and into a large bowl.

6. Allow the broth to cool then skim off the top fatty layer and discard (see page 232). Keep the broth in the refrigerator until ready to use.

EXPERT TIPS

* Freeze the broth in single serving portions so that you have some ready made whenever you need it.

* If you want extra flavor in the broth, you can add some rough chopped garlic to the pot when you add the other vegetables.

* It's important to strain through a fine strainer to achieve a really silky smooth broth.

191 BROWN BROTH

This broth is prepared in a slightly different way to chicken broth. For this technique the bones are roasted in the oven to concentrate the flavors first, before being transferred to the stove to simmer with the other ingredients.

TOOLS AND INGREDIENTS

Roasting pan
Sharp chef's knife
Cutting board
Large pot
Skimming spoon or large flat spoon
Fine strainer
Large bowl
3 lbs (1.35 kg) beef and/or veal bones
1 onion
2 carrots
2 celery stalks
5 whole black peppercorns
1 bouquet garni (see page 62)

METHOD

1 Preheat the oven to 450°F (230°C).

2 Put approximately 3 pounds (1.35 kg) of beef and/or veal bones into a large roasting pan. Spread the bones out so they are in a single layer and roast in the oven for 20 minutes.

3. Remove from the oven and add 1 onion, 2 carrots, 2 celery stalks, all rough chopped, to the pan, with a splash of water. Return to the oven and roast for a further 20 minutes.

4. Transfer the bones and vegetables into a large pot and add 12½ cups (3 liters) of cold water, 5 whole black peppercorns and 1 bouquet garni (see page 62).

5. Bring to a boil and simmer for 3–4 hours. Using a skimming spoon, or large flat spoon, skim the surface of the broth frequently to remove the scum.

6. Strain the broth through a fine strainer and into a large bowl.

7. Allow the broth to cool then skim off the top fatty layer and discard. Keep the broth in the refrigerator until ready to use.

EXPERT TIPS

* If you crack the bones before you roast them, they will release even more flavor.

* Brown broth is extremely rich – just a little added to pasta dishes, stews or sauces can really enrich the flavor. If you freeze the broth in ice cube trays (see page 233) you can add as little or as much as you need to a dish without having to defrost more than you need.

192 VEGETABLE BROTH

A good homemade vegetable broth should be a store-cupboard staple – stored in single serving batches in the freezer ready for use in risottos, soups or stews at a moment's notice.

METHOD

1. Put 4½ pounds (2 kg) of rough chopped onions, carrots, celery and leeks in a large pot and add 6 whole black peppercorns and 1 bouquet garni (see page 62).

2. Add 8½ cups (2 liters) of cold water to the pot and bring to a boil. Simmer the broth for 1 hour.

3. Strain through a fine strainer into a large bowl.

TOOLS AND INGREDIENTS

Sharp chef's knife
Cutting board
Large pot
Fine strainer
Large bowl

4½ lbs (2 kg) chopped onions, carrots, celery and leeks
6 whole black peppercorns
1 bouquet garni (see page 62)

EXPERT TIPS

* For a richer flavor, fry the vegetables in butter before adding them to the pot.

193 FISH BROTH

Whether you're making a fish stew, or a luxurious seafood risotto, it will be much improved by the addition of home-cooked fish broth. It's very easy to make, just requiring time for the flavors to infuse.

METHOD

1. Put 2 bay leaves, 8 whole black peppercorns, 1 onion, 1 carrot and 1 celery stalk, all quartered, a bouquet garni (see page 62) and 1 pound 2 ounces (500 g) of cleaned, mixed fish bones and trimmings, and a fish head (if you can get one) into a large pot.

2. Add 10½ cups (2.5 liters) of cold water and 1 cup (240 ml) of white wine (optional).

3. Bring to a boil and simmer for 30 minutes, skimming frequently (see page 232).

4. Strain the broth through a fine strainer into a large bowl. Use immediately or leave to cool and store in the refrigerator, tightly covered.

TOOLS AND INGREDIENTS

Large pot	1 onion
Sharp chef's knife	1 carrot
Cutting board	1 celery stalk
Skimming spoon	1 bouquet garni (see page 62)
Fine strainer	1 lb 2 oz (500 g) mixed fish
Large bowl	bones and trimmings
2 bay leaves	1 cup (240 ml) white wine
8 whole peppercorns	(optional)

EXPERT TIPS

* If you choose to add wine to the broth, don't use the cheapest cooking wine you can find. Wine adds flavor and it's worth spending a little more on a quality wine.

194 SKIMMING BROTHS

When the broth is simmering, a lot of scum rises to the surface. This is fat and other matter from the bones and sinew and it needs to be removed. It will look frothy in appearance and it is easily skimmed off the surface by using a special skimming spoon, or any large flat spoon. Alternatively, you can use sheets of paper towel to remove the top layer.

METHOD

1 Most broth recipes take a number of hours of gentle simmering in order for the ingredients to infuse and the flavor to intensify. At intervals, check on the broth and when you see the frothy scum collect on the surface, use a skimming spoon or slotted spoon to remove this layer.

2 Slide the spoon just underneath the scum layer and drag it across the surface, collecting the layer in the spoon. Remove and discard. You might have to do this two or three times and then repeat throughout the cooking time.

TOOLS AND INGREDIENTS

Pot of broth
Paper towel
Skimming spoon or
  slotted spoon

EXPERT TIPS

* Alternatively, when the pot has been removed from the heat and the broth is still hot, pass a double-folded paper towel through it. The paper will absorb any fat. This method works well for meat broths. You can use this method as well as skimming with a spoon.

* If you are making broth in advance, allow it to cool then chill it in the refrigerator. Once cold, the fat will solidify on the surface and can be carefully scooped off in pieces.

195 FREEZING BROTH CUBES

This is a great way to keep a constant supply of broth in small batches. You can then simply remove the amount you need without having to defrost a whole batch.

TOOLS AND INGREDIENTS

Ice cube trays
Broth

METHOD

1 When the cooked broth has been cooked, set aside and cool, carefully pour into clean ice cube trays.

2 Transfer to the freezer and keep flat. Once frozen, you can either leave the cubes in the tray or put them in sealed freezer bags or containers.

EXPERT TIPS

* The broth will expand slightly when frozen so don't fill the trays right up to the rim.

233

196 CLARIFYING BROTH

Clarifying basically means to make a liquid clear and this method is used to make broths and other clear soups and sauces that need to be completely strained of solids.

TOOLS AND INGREDIENTS

Balloon whisk
Mixing bowl
Fine strainer
Cheesecloth
3 egg whites
2 tbsp (30 ml) lemon
 juice
12 oz (350 g) mirepoix
 (see expert tips
 opposite)
8½ cups (2 L) warm
 broth

METHOD

1. Beat 3 egg whites in a scrupulously clean bowl until frothy. Add 2 tablespoons (30 ml) lemon juice and approximately 12 ounces (350 g) mirepoix (see expert tips).

2. Add the mixture to 8½ cups (2 liters) warm broth, and bring to a boil. Beat constantly until a crust forms – this will take about 4–6 minutes.

3. Make a hole in the crust for the broth to simmer through and simmer gently for 1 hour. Do not stir.

4. Line a fine strainer with damp cheesecloth and strain the broth through it into a large bowl. The resulting liquid should be translucent.

235

SPICE SKILLS

Spices take ordinary dishes and ingredients and turn them into the extraordinary. Without spices, food would be extremely plain and dull: spicing – whether subtle or obvious – adds another dimension to vegetable, meat and fish dishes.

There are different techniques used for extracting flavor from spices and this chapter will introduce you to the skills required to make the most of the exotic flavors that toasted, ground and soaked spices can add to different dishes. The way you prepare and cook individual spices makes a huge difference to the flavor they impart to food, so it's important to follow the guidelines in individual recipes, in order to make the most of these wonderful ingredients.

197 TOASTING SPICES

Many spices (such as cumin, mustard seeds and fennel seeds) benefit from being toasted before they are added to dishes. This preparation method releases the flavors, which will make a big difference to the finished dish. Smaller spices such as mustard seeds will begin to spot and sizzle when they are hot enough.

TOOLS AND INGREDIENTS

Small, heavy-based skillet
Spices
Dish or bowl

EXPERT TIPS

* Most spices will toast at about the same time so it is fine to add a variety of different whole spices to the hot pan together.

METHOD

1 Heat a small heavy-based skillet (there is no need to add any oil).

2 Once hot, add the whole chosen spices (according to the recipe or personal preference) and toast them over the heat until they begin to smell fragrant. Do not let the spices darken or burn.

3 When cooked, remove the skillet from the heat and transfer the spices to a dish or bowl so they stop cooking. You can now add them whole to the recipe or grind them (see opposite).

198 GRINDING SPICES

Nothing quite compares to the smell of freshly ground spices. This technique is used to get a fine powder for sauces, curries or spice pastes, where the consistency has to be smooth.

METHOD

1. Toast the selection of spices that you are going to use (see opposite).

2. Place the toasted spices in a pestle and mortar and grind them in a pounding and circular motion until you have a fine powder. This will take a little while in order to achieve a fine, even powder. You can use a teaspoon to move the spice mixture around the mortar occasionally, in order to get an even mix.

3. Alternatively, place the toasted spices in a coffee or spice grinder and blend until they resemble a fine powder.

EXPERT TIPS

* Although it is good to keep jars of your most used ground spices in the cupboard, freshly ground spices offer a far superior flavor and aroma. The flavor of spices in jars will gradually deteriorate over time.

* Make a large batch of ground spices and keep them in small, sealed containers for use in future recipes.

TOOLS AND INGREDIENTS

Pestle and mortar or
  coffee/spice grinder
Spices
Teaspoon (optional)

199 SOAKING SAFFRON

As the most expensive spice in the world, saffron should be used carefully and treated with respect. Despite its hefty price tag, it will be money well spent, as you only need a tiny pinch of this rich, pungent spice to transform a dish.

METHOD

1. Place a pinch of saffron strands in a small heatproof bowl.

2. Pour over enough boiling water to fully cover all of the strands but not too much or the flavor will be diluted.

3. Leave the saffron to stand for 10–15 minutes.

4. Strain the liquid through a fine strainer over another small bowl to use for cooking. It should be a vibrant orange/amber color.

TOOLS AND INGREDIENTS

Small heatproof bowl
Fine strainer
Small bowl
Pinch of saffron

EXPERT TIPS

* Saffron comes from the dried stigma of a crocus. It is expensive because collecting the stigma is a labor-intensive job — they can only be picked by hand.

* Use saffron stamens, or saffron liquid, in risottos, paellas, tagines and Indian dishes.

200 USING A VANILLA BEAN

Vanilla is another expensive spice that should be used carefully. Luckily, although the seeds inside the bean offer the intense flavor, the empty beans can also be used to infuse dishes.

TOOLS AND INGREDIENTS

Small, sharp chef's knife
Cutting board
Small paring knife

Small dish (optional)
Vanilla bean

EXPERT TIPS

* Once the seeds of the vanilla bean have been used, the bean can be kept and used for subtle flavoring. Simply put the empty bean into a jar of sugar or add it to custard or other sauces while cooking, and it will infuse the ingredient or dish with a rich, yet subtle, vanilla flavor.

* Use vanilla to flavor custard, cream, cakes and biscuits or savory fish and shellfish dishes.

* Some cooks find vanilla extract or paste more convenient to use. However, do not use vanilla essence as its flavor is inferior.

METHOD

1. Halve the vanilla bean by cutting it in half lengthwise. Lay the halves of the bean on a cutting board so the seeds are facing upward.

2. Using a small paring knife, scrape out the seeds from each half, pressing down fairly hard on the bean in order to extract all the seeds, but without cutting through the bean.

3. You can add the seeds directly to the dish, or scrape them off the knife onto a small dish, to use when ready.

GLOSSARY OF INGREDIENTS

Agar agar
This is the vegetarian alternative to gelatin. It is extracted from sea vegetables.

Arugula
Peppery leaves that can be wild or cultivated, it adds flavor and interest to salad, and can also be used as a garnish for pizza and pasta dishes.

Asian (kaffir) lime leaves
Vibrant leaves with a tangy citrus taste that are used in Asian dishes to add depth of flavor.

Aspic
A clear jelly that can contain gelatin. It is made from meat, chicken, or fish broth.

Baking powder
A raising agent used in baking. It contains alkali (cream of tartar) and acid (sodium bicarbonate).

Basil
There are many varieties of basil, and Genovese – or sweet basil – is the most common. It has a mild anise flavor. Thai (holy) basil is used in Asian cooking.

Bay leaf
Can be used fresh, or dried (for example in a bouquet garni). Bay adds depth of flavor, but it is strong so use sparingly.

Baking soda
A raising agent that is used when there are acidic ingredients in a dish.

Bonito flakes
These salty flakes are dried fermented tuna flakes that are mainly used in Japanese cooking.

Buckwheat
Brown, triangular grain that is good toasted, and can be made into porridge and flour.

Buttermilk
Made from fermented low-fat milk with a slightly sour flavor. Used in baking, for recipes such as soda bread.

Charcuterie
A term used to describe cured meats such as salami, Parma ham, and pâtés.

Cheddar cheese
A variety of strong English cheese from the Somerset village of the same name. Longer aged Cheddars have a sharp taste; good for melting and shredding.

Cilantro
A delicate herb with a peppery, lemony flavor. Finely chop the leaves and stalks and add towards the end of cooking or use as a garnish.

Clotted cream
Rich, thick cream with a high fat content and a slightly sweet flavor.

Coconut milk (coconut cream)
Made from the grated meat of the coconut (coconut water is the liquid inside), coconut milk is available in liquid or block form. It should be added toward the end of cooking so it doesn't split or curdle. It adds a creamy texture and taste to dishes and is used widely in Asian cookery.

Corn syrup
A thick, sweet syrup processed from cornstarch. Comes in light and dark forms. Dark corn syrup has a rich caramel flavor.

Cornstach
Coarse type of flour that is ground from the white starch of maize kernel. It is used as a thickening agent when mixed with cold water and added to dishes such as sauces and soups.

Cornmeal
Coarse flour made from dried maize.

Crème fraîche
A soured cream with a high fat content, this ingredient is good for cooking as it doesn't curdle.

Curry leaves
Curry leaves have a musky citrus flavor and tend to be fried or added whole to curry dishes.

Dill
A herb with an anise lemon flavor, dill works particularly well with fish. The seeds can also be toasted and are good with pork.

Frangipane
Buttery almond paste that is used in baking – either as a filling or as a base for other ingredients.

Game
Wild animals and birds that are shot to be eaten (rather than being reared domestically), such as pheasant and venison.

Garbanzo beans
A legume that has a slight nutty flavor. Garbanzos are widely used in Middle Eastern and Indian cooking. Available canned or dried: if dried, soak overnight and boil in fresh water until cooked.

Ghee
An Indian diary product – clarified and cooked butter. Ghee has a higher burning point than butter, which makes it a good choice good for sautéing. It also has a nutty flavor that can add depth to dishes.

Giblets
The gizzard, heart, neck, and liver of poultry. These are good for making broth.

Ginger
This root has many uses and comes in many varieties – stem, fresh, crystallized, ground. It has numerous uses across both savory and sweet recipes.

Honey
Varieties vary with bee species, flower species, region, and country. The honey can take on the essence of the flowers, and the darker the color, the richer and sweeter the flavor.

Horseradish
A root with a sharp hot flavor. It can be kept in the freezer and used as needed. Good minced.

Hot sauce (such as Tabasco)
There are many varieties of hot spicy sauces made from red pepper, chili flakes, and vinegar. Just a few drops can add a kick to any dish.

Jicama
Also known as a Mexican turnip, this crunchy, juicy vegetable is similar to an apple. Peel off the skin before using and eat it raw or cooked.

Lemongrass
A tropical species of grass, the stalk of this plant has a strong lemony flavor. Remove tough outer leaves then bruise the stalk before using it whole or finely chopped.

Lentils
Choose from puy, green, yellow, red, and split pea. Lentils are pulses that are used to add bulk and texture to dishes.

Maple syrup
Produced from the sap of the maple tree, this syrup has a dark, rich flavor that makes it ideal for baking.

Marjoram
A delicate, soft-leaved herb with a citrus flavor. It doesn't benefit from being overcooked, so it is best added at the end of cooking.

Mascarpone
This Italian soft cream cheese, has a mild flavor and can be used in pasta dishes or sweet recipes.

Mint
A hardy herb with fresh flavor. It is best added after cooking, but can be used fresh or dried also good. Also used to make tea.

Mirin
This sweet alcohol is made from fermented rice. It has a strong and salty flavor and is used in Japanese cuisine.

Molasses (black treacle)
A thick syrup that is the by-product of refining sugar. It has a strong, deep flavor and often used in ginger cakes and other baked recipes.

Mustard
There are many varieties, including English, whole-grain, Dijon, and brown. Mustard can be used as a base ingredient for dressings and also adds a peppery flavor to dishes.

Nori
Thin, dried sheets of seaweed that is mainly used for wrapping sushi as it has a mild taste.

Nutmeg
This spice has a warm flavor and is used in savory and sweet dishes. It is best grated fresh into the dish.

Oil
Choose from an extensive selection including olive, vegetable, canola, and sunflower oil, which are all good for cooking. Other oils such as walnut, argan, sesame, peanut, and flax are betting for adding flavor. You can make homemade flavored oils by adding garlic, chili, truffle, or herbs to bottles of olive oil.

Oregano
This peppery herb is widely used in Greek, Italian, and Mexican cooking – fresh and dried.

Parmesan
A hard Italian cheese that contains rennet. It is aged for minimum 6 months and is used in pasta and rice dishes and grated over food before serving.

Parsley
Choose form flat leaf or curly varieties. It, works well as a garnish and in a bouquet garni. It is a versatile herb as it doesn't have an overpowering flavor.

Pepperoncino
These dried chili flakes add extra heat during cooking.

Polenta
This North Italian staple is a type of cornmeal that can be prepared soft (similar in consistency to mashed potato) or set and sliced to serve.

Pomegranate syrup (molasses)
A thick, tangy, and sweet syrup that is made from concentrated pomegranate juice.

Porcini
These strong mushrooms have a delicate, earthy flavor. Dried porcini need to be soaked in hot water to rehydrate.

Prosciutto
A variety of dry-cured Italian ham. There are regional varieties such as Parma and San Daniele.

Rosemary
A tough woody herb that is best cooked. Its strong flavor works particularly well with lamb.

Ricotta
This soft Italian cheese is made from re-cooked whey. It has a mild taste and is the famous partner for spinach, often used as a pizza topping or pasta filling.

Rye
Strong flour with a dark taste and color, used for bread.

Sage
A herb with soft, velvety leaves and a musky flavor. The favorite choice for stuffing recipes and it also works well to compliment fatty foods.

Sea Beans

This salty, crunchy sea vegetable needs to be rinsed thoroughly before use. It is best steamed or blanched and goes well with fish and shellfish dishes.

Semolina

Pale yellow flour that is made from durum wheat. It works well in sweet milk puddings and is also an ingredient in dried pasta.

Shallot

A member of the onion family – shallots are smaller and have a sweeter flavor. Can be eaten raw or cooked.

Soy sauce

Made from fermented soya beans and available in light and dark varieties. Tamari (dark but not too salty) soy sauce has a lighter flavor. Both are salty so there is no need to add extra salt to the dish.

Scallion (green onion)

These long, thin stems are often used as a garnish, particularly in Asian cuisine. Their mild flavor means they are good raw.

Star anise

A warm spice with fennel and anise flavors. Use whole in curries and stews to add flavor.

Sugar

Many varieties, including white, superfine, and granulated, dark and light brown, and confectioner's. Each has a specific culinary use.

Tahini

A creamy paste made from ground sesame seeds, tahini is the base ingredient in hummus and is used as flavoring in Middle Eastern cuisine.

Tamarind

This is derived from the pods of the tamarind tree and is usually available as a paste. It has a sour citrus taste.

Tarragon

A delicate herb with an anise flavor. Partners well with chicken and beef dishes.

Thyme

Available in regular or lemon varieties, this woody herb with its earthy flavor benefits from long cooking.

Vanilla

These contain seeds of an orchid plant and it is best to buy whole beans and scrape out the seeds. Also available in extract, which is mainly used for baking.

Vinegar

A whole range of vinegars are available, including apple cider, white and red wine, and balsamic, which has a rich, deep flavor.

Wasabi

A potent relation to horseradish, wasabi has a very strong peppery taste. Available as a pale green powder or paste and it is often served with sushi.

White radish

An oriental radish with crisp white flesh. Can be used raw and pickled, it has a subtle peppery flavor.

Yeast

A raising agent used in bread, yeast is available dried or fresh.

Yogurt

Available natural, flavored or Greek. Cow's milk yogurt is the most common, but you can also use sheep or goats' milk yogurt. When unflavored, it is thick with a slight sourness.

Za'atar

A spice blend of salt, sesame seeds, and za'atar thyme. Used widely in Middle Eastern cuisine.

DICTIONARY OF TERMS

Acidulate
Adding lemon juice (eg. to water) to prevent discoloring when left cut.

Al dente
Italian term to describe pasta/vegetables cooked to the point when they retian a slight bite to texture.

Baking blind
Pre-baking a pastry case by lining with baking paper and filling with baking/dried beans.

Bain marie
A deep dish/pot/container half filled with hot water with a dish set either on top or in water. Used for melting chocolate, cooking soufflé, etc. It creates a moist, steamy environment for the oven or stove.

Bard
Wrapping low fat meat, game, or poultry in thin layer of fat to keep it moist while cooking.

Baste
Spooning juices over meat during cooking to prevent it from drying.

Bind
Adding a roux, eggs, or butter to a dry mix to blend and hold it together.

Blanch
To boil fruits, vegetables, or nuts, etc. briefly to cook and loosen skin.

Bone
To remove bones from meat, poultry, game, or fish.

Bouquet garni
A bunch of fresh herbs such as parsely, thyme, and bay used to flavor during cooking.

Braise
Cooking slowly in liquid inside the oven.

Brine
This is a salt and water solutuon used to pickle.

Bruise
Crushing an ingredient to release flavor and fragrance in cooking.

Brule
Adding a crsip caramelized sugar top.

Butterfly
Partially cutting a piece of meat open to make it flatter and decrease cooking time.

Caramelize
Heating sugar until it becomes a syrup

Ceviche
Raw fish "cooked" in lime or lemon juice.

Chine
This is a procedure to separate ribs from backbone.

Choux pastry
A form of cooked pastry used in profiteroles and other filled patisserie.

Clarify
To heat and filter fats in order to to make them clear.

Compôte
A soft mixture of cooked fruits.

Concasse
A term that simply means "roughly diced."

Confit
Meat cooked slowly in fat over a long period and then stored in the fat.

Coulis
A thin, runny fruit purée used as a sauce or garnish for desserts such as meringue.

Court bouillon
A poaching liquid, for example to poach fish.

Cream
A term meaning to beat butter and sugar together to incorporate air into the mixture until it is pale and fluffy.

Cure
Preserving food with salt, brine, or smoke.

Deglaze
Adding a liquid, such as wine, to a pan that has had meat cooked in it to make sauce.

Degrease
Removing grease from a liquid, such as fat from gravy. Can chill the liquid so that the fat hardens and then it can be lifted off, or you can skim off with a spoon while still hot.

Dropping consistency
A mixture that will hold its shape but drop off a spoon.

Emulsify
To whisk two liquids together, such as oil and vinegar.

En croute
This term simply means "in pastry."

Fold
To gently mix a light mixture into a heavy one, avoiding knocking out the air.

Fry
To cook in hot fat Deep frying means the food is submerged. Shallow frying means it is just coated.

Fumet
An intensely flavored, concentrated broth.

Fusion cooking
Combining flavors and methods from different cuisines and countries.

Glaze
Brushing with thin liquid that leaves a glossy coating.

Gnocchi
Small dumplings made from potato or semolina.

Gratin
When a dish is topped with cheese, breadcrumbs, and then baked or grilled.

Grease
To coat or line baking ware with butter or oil to prevent sticking.

Griddle
A heavy cast iron pan with ridges that marks food cooked on it with appealing lines.

Hull
To remove stalks or tops of fruit such as strawberries.

Infuse
Adding flavor by steeping with a fragrant ingredient.

Knead
Working dough to make it firm and smooth and release gluten.

Knock back
Pushing risen dough back to knock the air out so it collapses.

Larding
To insert fat into a lean meat to add moisture when it is cooked.

Liason
A mixture of egg yolk and cream added to sauces and stews to thicken.

Macerate
Soaking fruit in a liquid or syrup to soften and intensify its flavor.

Marbling
The delicious lines of fat throughout cuts of meat.

Marinade
To soak meats in a mixture of seasonings to intensify flavor, add moisture, and tenderize the meat.

Mirepoix
A term that simply means, "finely diced."

Par boil or par cook
To cook partially until slightly underdone and then finish later or with a different method. Potatoes, for example, are par boiled before roasting.

Pectin
The natural setting agent fruits and vegetables.

Pith
This is the slightly bitter white lining between the flesh and skin of citrus fruits.

Poach
Cooking in an almost boiling liquid, works well for fish.

Pot roast
Cooking meat in a covered pot inside the oven with very little or no liquid.

Purée
A smooth, blended and sifted food.

Quenelle
This term means "oval shape." It can refer to dumplings or items like poached mousse for fish.

Ragout
A slow-cooked meat sauce.

Reduce
To concentrate a liquid by boiling it, reduce the quantity and intensifing its flavor.

Refresh
Quickly cooling cooked vegetables by placing them into ice cold water to keep their bright color.

Render
Cooking meat to release or reduce its fat.

Roux
A mixture of cooked flour and butter in equal quantities. It is a base for white sauces and thickens.

Sashimi
Thin slices of raw fish used in sushi.

Sauté
To fry quickly in hot oil or butter.

Scald
To heat to just boiling point or to plunge a fruit or vegetable into boiling water to remove skins.

Score
Making incisions on skin of meat before cooking.

Sear
Browning meat to color without cooking through, just to seal in the juices.

Simmer
To cook in liquid that is just below boiling point.

Skim
Removing scum from the surface using a large spoon.

Steam
Cooking over simmering water in a sealed pot to hold in the moisture.

Steep
Soaking in liquid to absorb flavor, or rehydrating dried foods such as mushrooms.

Stir fry
Cooking quickly over very high heat, often in a wok.

Sweat
To cook gently a over low heat to soften.

Truss
Tying with string to keep in shape, such as a whole chicken or joint.

Whisk
Adding air to a mixture by beating with whisk.

RESOURCES

Shopping at independent stores and farmers' markets is rewarding. Get to know your butcher, fishmonger, deli owner and grocer. If possible, buy organic meat and fish from sustainable sources (visit www.fishwatch.gov for more information). Here are some online stores which help you.

Butchers
Meathub
www.meathub.com

Blues Creek Farm Meats
www.bluescreekfarmmeats.com

Home Grown Cow
www.homegrowncow.com

Fishmongers
Farm 2 Market
www.farm-2-market.com

All Fresh Seafood
www.allfreshseafood.com

Giovanni's Fish Market
www.giovannisfishmarket.com

The Seattle Fish Company
www.seattlefishcompany.com

Oils, spices etc.
Glaser Organic Farms
www.glaserorganicfarms.com

The Spice House
www.thespicehouse.com

My Spice Sage
www.myspicesage.com

The Savory Spice Shop
www.savoryspiceshop.com

Kalustyans
www.kalustyans.com

Penzeys
www.penzeys.com

Greengrocers and Markets
The Shet Shop
www.chefshop.com

From the Farm
www.fromthefarm.com
Fruit Share
www.fruitshare.com

Eat Wikd
www.eatwild.com

Cheese and deli items
Dean and Deluca
www.deananddeluca.com

Murray's Cheese
www.murrayscheese.com

Cheese Supply
www.cheesesupply.com
Di Bruno Bros
www.dibruno.com

Zabar's
www.zabars.com

Gourmet Food Store
www.gourmetfoodstore.com

Artisanal Premium Cheese
www.artisanalcheese.com

Cowgirl Creamery
www.cowgirlcreamery.com

Zingerman's
www.zingermans.com

Baking equipment and ingredients
N.Y. Cake
www.nycake.com

Pastry Items
www.pastryitems.com

Will Powder
www.willpowder.net

Marque Foods
www.marquefoods.com

King Arthur Flour
www.kingarthurflour.com

Kitchen Krafts
www.kitchenkrafts.com

Sasa Demarle
www.demarleusa.com

Kitchen Equipment
Kitchen Aid
www.kitchenaid.com

Magimix
www.magimix.com

Kenwood
www.kenwood.com

Sur la Table
www.surlatable.com

Crate & Barrel
www.crateandbarrel.com

The Gourmet Depot
www.thegourmetdepotco.com

Bed, Bath & Beyond
www.bedbathandbeyond.com

Williams-Sonoma
www.williams-sonoma.com

CONVERSION CHARTS

WEIGHTS

Pounds & Ounces	Kilograms & Grams
½ oz	10 g
¾ oz	20 g
1 oz	25 g
1½ oz	40 g
2 oz	50 g
2½ oz	60 g
3 oz	75 g
4 oz	110 g
4½ oz	125 g
5 oz	150 g
6 oz	175 g
7 oz	200 g
8 oz	225 g
9 oz	250 g
10 oz	275 g
12 oz	350 g
1 lb	450 g
1 lb 8 oz	700 g
2 lb	900 g
3 lb	1.35 kg

DIMENSIONS

Inches	Centimeters & Millimeters
⅛ inch	3 mm
¼ inch	5 mm
½ inch	1 cm
¾ inch	2 cm
1 inch	2.5 cm
1¼ inch	3 cm
1½ inch	4 cm
1¾ inch	4.5 cm
2 inch	5 cm
2½ inch	6 cm
3 inch	7.5 cm
3½ inch	9 cm
4 inch	10 cm
5 inch	13 cm
5½ inch	13.5 cm
6 inch	15 cm
6½ inch	16 cm
7 inch	18 cm
7½ inch	19 cm
8 inch	20 cm
9 inch	23 cm
9½ inch	24 cm
10 inch	25.5 cm
11 inch	28 cm
12 inch	30 cm

VOLUMES

Cups & Fluid Ounces	Liters and Milliliters
2 fl oz	55 ml
3 fl oz	75 ml
5 fl oz	150 ml
10 fl oz	275 ml
1 cup	240 ml
4¼ cups	1 liter

Spoons	Milliliters
½ teaspoon	3 ml
1 teaspoon	5 ml
1 tablespoon	15 ml

OVEN TEMPERATURES

°F	°C
275°F	140°C
300°F	150°C
325°F	170°C
350°F	180°C
375°F	190°C
400°F	200°C
425°F	220°C
450°F	230°C
475°F	240°C

If using a convection oven you will need to reduce the oven temperature in a recipe by 20°F (10°C).

WEIGHT CONVERSIONS

	Ounces	Grams
1 cup flour	5 oz	150 g
1 cup white/ superfine sugar	8 oz	225 g
1 cup brown sugar	6 oz	175 g
1 cup butter/margarine/ lard	8 oz	225 g
1 cup raisins	7 oz	200 g
1 cup currants	5 oz	150 g
1 cup ground almonds	4 oz	110 g
1 cup light corn syrup	12 oz	350 g
1 cup uncooked rice	7 oz	200 g
1 cup grated cheese	4 oz	110 g
1 stick butter	4 oz	110 g

LIQUID CONVERSIONS

Fluid Ounces	Milliliters	Cups & Tablespoons
½ fl oz	15 ml	1 tbsp
1 fl oz	30 ml	⅛ cup
2 fl oz	60 ml	¼ cup
4 fl oz	120 ml	½ cup
8 fl oz	240 ml	1 cup

INDEX

ACKNOWLEDGMENTS

The authors would like to thank the following companies for their cooperation and assistance in providing equipment for this book.

Divertimenti
www.divertimenti.co.uk

George Wilkinson
www.george-wilkinson.com

Kitchen Craft
(+44 0)121 604 6000
www.kitchencraft.co.uk
www.facebook.com/
kitchencraftUK,
www.twitter.com/kitchencraft

Mermaid
www.mermaidcookware.com

OXO
www.oxo.com, www.oxouk.com

ProCook
www.procook.co.uk

Tala
www.talacooking.com